818 SW 3RD AVENUE #126, PORTLAND, OR 97204

GET ALIGNED NOW

Free Your Mind Through Body Intelligence

The Path To Achieve Aligned Results.

BETHANY LONDYN

COPYRIGHT

Although the author and publisher have made every effort to ensure that the information in this book was acceptable at press time, they reserve the right to alter and update the opinions expressed.

The material in this book reflects a personal perspective. It is not intended to be a substitute for professional or psychological advice. This book provides information used for entertainment and self-development purposes.

Some names used throughout the book have been changed for confidentiality reasons. The author and publisher do not assume and hereby disclaim any liability to any party for any loss, damage, or disruption caused.

FREE RESOURCES

To enjoy the free resources that accompany this book, please visit Londyn's site and consult the Get Aligned Now section.

http://www.bethanylondyn.com/getalignednow

REASONS TO READ THIS BOOK

You are yearning for more clarity in your life.

You are looking for tips for re-calibrating your life and finding balance.

You are ready to stop living a chaotic lifestyle and wish to start regularly experiencing harmony and bliss.

You want to find out what your life purpose is.

You want to learn how to make the best decisions.

You would like to accomplish your goals (especially your New Year's resolutions).

You are looking for support for getting through hardship.

You are looking to find balance in your inner life, between your mind and body.

You are looking to overcome the feeling of being disconnected from everything.

TABLE OF CONTENTS

ACKNOWLEDGMENTS

Writing and birthing this beautiful book has been a labor of love. I must acknowledge those who have been part of my momentum.

First and foremost, I want to acknowledge God for the inspiration to write this book, and a huge shout out to my past hardships. I would not have been able to write this had it not been for the demanding situations and trying people I've encountered, and who ultimately supported my journey. Learning the lessons from these situations, I was able to craft the message of this book, in order to assist others in avoiding unnecessary turbulence.

I am grateful to Ruben for nudging me to finish the book, along with my friends and family, who have continually been my cheerleaders and feedback givers. To name a few: Mom, Dad, Cara, Amy, Granny, Lydia, Julien, Sergio, Cristin, Jeffrey, Susie, Tessie, Jade, & Cyndi. I also am including my high vibing furry family, my dogs Kessler and Elliot as part of the tribe of phenomenal beings who have surrounded me, making my life a brighter place along this journey. Lastly, a special thanks to my editor Eva who put me through the ringers to bring to light a better version of my work. I am very fortunate and blessed.

INTRODUCTION

MY MISSION:

I intend to empower you to learn from all that your body is sharing. In carrying out the breakthrough of listening, through presence to yourself vs. others, you may become fluent in the flow of life, thus getting aligned to results via your body's intelligence, an expansion upon emotional intelligence.

I am an Alignment Catalyst, and people always ask how I achieve results with my clients. This recurring question gave rise to the idea "Hey, maybe it's time for me to expand upon my circle and share with the world." Therefore, this book is foundational and serves a passion of mine to help people reach clarity and re-define their life journeys. Many people feel trapped in the chaos of their lives, and I want everyone to find personal freedom through clarity and the choices they make every day.

I have found immense peace and a sense of calmness within myself through the steps presented in this book. Even during my toughest life struggles and challenges, I understand now that I had a choice to embrace it all. Yes, you read that right, a CHOICE, albeit a subconscious choosing of struggle.

Many people live from fear, a life that depends on others for self-worth, love, and direction. Many people go to the gym because they fear being fat or because they can't stand the way they look, instead of loving their body enough to honor it through a workout. Do you see the perspective twist? This low vibrating energy is what causes conflict and a feeling of entrapment that carries on throughout the rest of your daily activities.

Empowering yourself to grasp the difference through feeling and listening, engaging with peace and love, and a constant knowing that you have all the tools in your body to proceed in the highest and best path is what we're going to do. You're increasing your vibration as you learn to live from the foundation, honoring your truth. This truth within that you may not even be aware of just yet, but wait, it's coming! This book will enable you to uncover your truth, thus allowing you to gain personal freedom by owning your inner voice and the God within.

Here's the problem: people always think that they need to listen to someone else, learn from someone else, and follow someone else to get to where they want to go in life. STOP! There is another way, and it's surprisingly easy, once you get the hang of it.

People pay tons of money for therapy, counselors, etc. I'm a coach, so I'm all for an investment in yourself, yet it is still most important to listen to the truths that exist within. When we get present and tap into the bodies we've been gifted, we gain universal knowledge and learn to guide ourselves. We learn to stop listening, or caring for that matter, to what others think, because the answers are right inside!

Let's get started with a couple of definitions to support you throughout:

WHAT IS ALIGNMENT?

Alignment is the connection between your thoughts, goals, desires, and your actual life. It is the intersection of your inner world and the outer reality, the line that links your past, present and future on your life's map.

When in the energy of alignment, you open yourself up to life in a state of ease and flow. This state allows that which you wish to achieve to manifest, with simplicity and joy. Your energy when in alignment is EVERYTHING. What you believe and are aware of is your truth, and you have the power to change what you see, know, and attract at any time. The power is in that present moment.

Clients often hold their goals above themselves on a pedestal, which means automatically they are not in alignment. I support clients getting on the same level of alignment with their goals so that they are attainable. The key ingredients for this process is Body Intelligence and joy.

> *"Follow your bliss.*
> *If you do follow your bliss,*
> *you put yourself on a kind of track*
> *that has been there all the while waiting for you,*
> *and the life you ought to be living*
> *is the one you are living.*
> *When you can see that,*
> *you begin to meet people*
> *who are in the field of your bliss,*
> *and they open the doors to you."*
> **— Joseph Campbell**

WHAT IS BODY INTELLIGENCE?

Body intelligence is the awareness and understanding of the physical and emotional responses communicated by our body.

Body intelligence allows you to align to your goals by finding answers and guidance within, releasing clouded judgment from past and external experiences, thus allowing your advice to come forth. Consider your body as your personal mentor.

Your body delivers feedback to questions, challenges, desires, and other people's influence. By becoming sensitive to this feedback, you become aware of new perspectives. Discover answers through your body, not only your mind. In simple terms, trust your gut. The body is continuously responding, positively or negatively, to guide you, and it's up to you to use this God-given birthright to your advantage. Consider it the source from where your intuition flows.

I'll share with you that at first, I had a hard time noticing my body's responses to anything. Whenever upsetting situations occurred, my coach would ask me "Where do you feel this in your body? What sensations are you experiencing?"

I had trouble answering him. I would physically freeze up every time. I instantly went numb, as there was a significant disconnect between my psyche and my body. It took me two years to fully become aware of my physical feelings, and to this day, it still is a daily practice. I am continually working on the discernment and experiences I'm feeling. Later, I'll share how this previous disconnection manifested into health issues and lead me to shut down a company.

In a parent's context, this could apply to deciding what school your child should go to, for example. Your choices are the public school within walking distance from your home, or a private school where all your child's friends are going. This decision is life-changing for many reasons, affecting your financial situation, your time (walking vs. driving), and the possibility of keeping or losing your child's friends. You want them to go to public school, but are getting a ton of flack from other parents about the fact that your kid isn't going to get the best education, that you're going to create problems by separating them from their friends, and that ultimately your child really should be in private school. This decision can create a lot of pressure. What do you do? Do you take on all the guilt, shame, and pressure from other people? This book will support you in finding the answer and knowing that you've made the perfect decision.

In a more light-hearted context, consider a woman who is interested in a guy and is concerned about what her friends might think of him, because he's over a decade older. As she uses the tools in this book, learns to trust herself, and listens to her body's natural guidance, she can find out if she should be with this guy or not. Once she's sure of her answer, she'll be confident in her decision and will let go of what her friends think.

Maybe you're working on a new startup project and have some critical decisions to make based on where interested investors feel you should pivot. They have a different vision than you, but is it the right one? You want to release attachment to the decision and make the best one for the livelihood of the company. Right? Once people block out the external noise, they can get to the heart of the matter, finding clarity and peace. Best of all, this guidance comes from their body. It's like having their own magic eight ball.

Using this internal guidance has supported my clients and myself with great fluidity and direction, from getting started in the morning and figuring out what the most productive tasks are for that day, to knowing when to walk away from a person who is an energy drain. You may already pick up on some of these experiences and not give them the weight they deserve. This book will allow you to own your truths, in a way you didn't think possible, and offer you many exciting truth-bombs.

Live by your truest self, unswayed by others opinions.

Each chapter of this book is a weekly program. Its structure mirrors an abundant, healthy tree, as our guide. I'll take you through relatable situations and offer activities and tools for growth. The weeks build upon each other to support you in your journey towards finding alignment to your truth and ultimately achieving your goals.

We use the tree as our metaphor because of its longevity, and its similarity to aspects of our physical, external, and spiritual Being- the infinite BEing that we are.

Did you watch the 2009 movie Avatar? It's one of my favorites, portraying how we are all connected and the vibrational energy that we consist of. The sketched out example sharing the energy of the tree and the beings, shows a beautiful perspective and lens that we can see the world from. Pretend you're looking at life through microscope vision and all you see is atoms bouncing around. You see the energy of everyone and everything', fluid and connecting.

We are called Human Beings. The Human aspect is the physical vessel that embodies the BEing, which is the essence of everything that we are.

Being encompasses the verb "Be", comprised of your spirit, soul, personality, and all that you have absorbed from your past experiences. This includes the stories made up about yourself from past and present situations, they all affect who you BE.

Here's a snippet of how the book is laid out using the vessel of the vibrant tree that is you:

THE EARTH, YOUR FOUNDATION

First, this book will guide you through your external environment. The first chapters will support finding clarity in your space, your living environment, and beyond. When your environment is in alignment, your body will at once feel the difference. These shifts will bring you to a more joyful and relaxed state.

THE ROOTS OF THE TREE, UNDERSTANDING YOU

Secondly, we will dive into the experience of your physical and emotional self. Fully connecting the two and getting clear will support awareness and create a new experience of the life you want now. We will tap into the conversations your body is having with you during everyday situations.

The book is a feeling experience, involving body talk and paying attention to the feels that your body is gifting you at every moment. Notice the ups and downs, along with any tightness and lightness. Your body's guidance is your birthright. The information your body shares is an underutilized reservoir of knowledge. Get excited; we will use frustration and anger to your advantage, on the journey to a happy, whole and aligned you.

THE TRUNK OF THE TREE, THE CORE

Thirdly, I will lead you towards creating your vision, most likely from a different angle than you have experienced before. You will manifest and achieve your goals with ease, by using your body's wisdom and guidance. Aligning with your vision via body intelligence supports your results beyond your imagination. Just the other day, a client reached phenomenal results -finding the house, work opportunity, and possibly the man she was looking for – thanks to the exercises we'll be doing in the coming weeks. She has achieved her results within only two months!

LEAVES, YOUR CONNECTION

Lastly, we'll dive into connection with the divine and the spiritual aspects of your life as a human BEing. The spirit of you knows your truth and can offer added insight, connecting you to untapped knowledge. Your intuition can come out and play with your physical being. The information stuck within your subconscious will support your movement forward, so that you can be fully aligned: mind, body, and soul.

Throughout the book, I will share my personal stories and guidance to support transformation in your life, whether you're a mom, a college student, a software engineer, or a CEO. Anyone can benefit from living a life of truth and alignment.

Get Aligned Now is meant as a resource for you to make entirely your own. When the guidance flows as clear as day, and you're resonating fully, you'll be seamlessly working towards alignment to your goals, through your newly discovered body intelligence.

I want you to know that this book is NOT a YOU MUST DO THIS OR ELSE book, nor it is a book about MAKING YOU WRONG about anything.

GETTING THE MOST FROM THIS BOOK

You may want to read through the entire book alone, then form an accountability group with friends or your book club, and go through each week together, or hop into one of our accountability groups online. You will tackle issues of everyday situations, and also get situated on your yellow brick road towards your goals.

When I read Katherine Woodward Thomas's book, *Calling in the One*, initially, I skimmed through it, thinking it seemed like a good book. Then, a couple of years later, a coaching friend asked me to hold her accountable for reading it each day. I decided to tag along and join her. Because we read the book together and sent each other notes on our takeaways each day, it not only had me taking a deeper dive, I was also hearing the experience she was having, which expanded my understanding of the material.

We all have lenses through which we grasp the lessons, and it's powerful to hear another's observations of the same material.

Each week we'll build upon the previous weeks' discoveries. You will learn the intuitive process of body alignment, as well as essential practices and activities to grow your awareness skill set. You will be asked questions to reflect upon, throughout the book, which will allow the communication with your Being to develop.

It is not a coincidence that you have picked up this book today. Your soul called for it, and you should be excited that it has! Things come to us at the perfect time, in various ways, whether we are prepared or not. As you'll learn throughout this book, awareness, followed by gratitude, is the key to everything. Paying attention and entering into a questioning state of curiosity, instead of frustration, can help you get through anything: from choosing which outfit to wear to deciding which person to hire or getting over relationship hurdles.

Now, you might wonder "Why is this Bethany person the one to educate me on body intelligence and alignment?" Just the other day, someone asked me if I was trying to play God as I shared that I had started working with cancer clients. No, absolutely not! I'm here delivering the information bestowed to me, and it's up to you to make it your own and use it towards clarity and inspired action.

I have learned and experienced many healing and coaching methods and am certified in some. Here are a few of my sources: God, Feng Shui, ThetaHealing(R), Reiki, Christianity, EFT, Ho'oponopono, Kundalini, Sozo, NLP (Neuro-linguistic programming), hypnosis, channeling, meditation, and the works of Dr. David R. Hawkins, Christie Marie Sheldon, Dr. Joe Dispenza, Joe Vitale, Napoleon Hill & Gabby Bernstein. This list is far from being complete.

What I have learned throughout my studies and training is that all these methods and approaches have similar processes that beautifully line up, especially when it comes to healing. Recently, I have been working with stage IV cancer patients. Throughout our sessions, some clients found instant relief for their ailments when we started uncovering their truths. Of the stage IV clients, a couple could all of a sudden breathe, whereas before they were having trouble. Others finally got a great night's sleep and many reached a state of clarity and forgiveness. Being aligned with our truth aids healing.

Interestingly enough, the healing and alignment methods previously listed are fundamentally very similar. However, I have noticed that any information we receive, as culturally different individuals, comes to us in unique ways that are perfect for us, so that we may best 'digest' them. For many, this book might be what you needed at this given moment; afterward, when you are feeling complete, you might take it to another level of exploration.

Know that this process is a journey. Let yourself experience the painful, sad, and even angry emotions that may arise – safely, of course. It will help you let go of the past and move towards the future you long for.

Whether you're reading this book and it's your introduction to this space, or it's your 22nd book in this genre, you will only retain what works for you and forget what doesn't resonate. Re-reading is a way to absorb information in its entirety, over time.

PAST
THE IMPORTANCE OF LISTENING
TO YOUR BODY

On May 1st, 2019, I left a real estate startup that I was involved with for just short of two years. I had fully committed myself to this company. I had worked seven days a week for almost two years, giving the company and my clients everything I had. In the last couple of months, before I finally left, I realized I had nothing left to give. The company was my priority. I put my clients first, and I put my public speaking, life coaching, and healing work on the back burner. I only did a few speaking gigs over those past two years, and the coaching & healing sessions performed were far and few between.

In those last couple of months, I was running on empty, on fumes. Always consumed by drama with the company, I was on an emotional roller coaster that would elevate my heart rate daily. Even though I was still continually facilitating miracles with my real estate clients, the fulfillment waned. One of the reasons it took me a long time to leave the company was my love for my clients. I couldn't imagine leaving them in the dust with someone who didn't care for them the way I did.

What started me on the journey with this company was the vision, the big dream. I was extremely excited to be a part of something so impactful in other countries — enticed by the enthusiasm of the people running the company and their commitment to our greatness.

Have you ever jumped into the unknown because of excitement?

Excitement supplies quite the rush and it is how many sales happen. My friends and family were trying to persuade me to choose a different path, and I felt they didn't understand. In fact, within a couple of weeks of starting this position, I left my boyfriend of a year. I no longer felt he had my back, and I most definitely didn't receive any support from him with my new company. You want to feel warm, cozy, and supported when in a partnership, right? Sometimes it's time to take note and shift gears, whether it's you or the both of you, when these feelings are no longer there. Part of the body intelligence mechanism is knowing your capacity, your limits and using the body for discernment when making decisions.

During my time at this company, I built protective walls around me regarding the backlash of others, and I thrived on the internal excitement of the company and my clients. They loved their experience with the company, and they loved their experience with me. My clients fueled me until I no longer felt valued, and my tank of energy and love went empty. In the beginning, I was a significant part of the creative process. In the end, everything I shared seemed to fall upon deaf ears.

Also, on May 1st, 2019, I began a relationship that is still evolving quite beautifully. I had shut one door, and another opened. It's like I only had the energy for one relationship during my time at the company,. The unconscious choosing was the relationship with the company. My bandwidth only allowed for alignment with one relationship at a time to which I take notice. Regardless of my personal capacity, the experiences still benefited me and allowed me to learn about myself. I left with many other positive outcomes as well, such as lessons, phenomenal friends, and loads of experience I wouldn't have gotten elsewhere at a startup.

One day, I visited one of my best friends, an influencer and conscientious mural artist, Ruben Rojas. As I sat on his couch in his art studio, he pulled the heartstrings right out of my chest, tears popping and all. I believe I was sharing about some of the healing work I had recently done with some cancer clients, and then he asked me "How could you possibly support healing others when you're running on empty, living a life not aligned to your truth?" My response was that when I was doing healing and coaching sessions, I felt tingly from head to toe filling me with revitalized energy. When I was living my truth and purpose, my body turned into vibrating electricity.

One of my earlier coaches used to share with me "You, Bethany, are the electricity that others plug into to shine their eternal light." It's so true. I physically experience this feeling inside. I feel the tingles when I'm preparing a talk, when I'm creating a workshop, as I write this book, when I am sharing a message from my heart with others, and when I'm doing coaching sessions.

When you are tingling inside, you are light, being in your truth. You are living your purpose, and most likely, in an experience of creating. I have found that people are happiest when they are in a creative process. We are all the light for each other, and sometimes we need to take a cloth and dust off the scum that's filtering it from shining its brightest! We are meant to live a life of joy and love. Following your happiness will allow you to lead a bliss-filled life. You are worthy of this experience, always.

When I jumped into that real estate company, I no longer could do the other things that I had previously been working on, such as writing this book, creating art, and coaching. I took a hiatus from everything I had been working on to jump ship into the unknown. Did I question my decisions? No. I jumped in regardless of discernment because I was excited about this vision. I don't have any regrets.

As I left Ruben's art studio, I had committed to him that by the end of the month, I would finish the first draft of my book. This passion project, which started almost four years ago, was more than 75% done! Nearly finished, yet apparently, I had been no longer inspired to finish it during those past two years. Jumping aboard this last company shifted me away from my vision of purpose. And that's okay, it was part of my journey.

Looking back, I can see how I allowed a vision to lead me, which is very powerful; however, it was not my vision, it was someone else's.

Whose vision are you living right now?

Do you feel the need for recalibration?

It's terrific supporting someone else's vision, as long as it coincides with yours as well. We will soon be addressing useful tools for aligning the two.

When I first said yes to becoming part of the startup, I wonder if I had checked my gut feeling and my body. Honestly, I don't remember. Excitement can be like a hypnotic drug and a phenomenal one at times. I believe following joy is the way to win with life. When you're not feeling it, something gets to shift.

When you are feeling frustrated, angry, disappointed, or upset - you are not in alignment. Think of a bad day: did you feel as though something was off? It was. You were not aligned. When in alignment, life flows effortlessly. You could be closer to living a life of bliss and joy. Not that the frustrations won't come, but you'll know how to navigate them and not allow them to weigh you down. These adverse experiences are great, as they expose you to the awareness that you are not in your truth. My goal is to get you to only the best days; and when you find yourself feeling off, you'll be able to acknowledge it and come back to these practices and align to your truth.

My truth found me at that real estate company, and it served me well. I gained valuable knowledge on getting a company and culture aligned to a vision. I found some long-lasting friendships. The joy was compelling and kept me going. However, when the gratification left and the knowledge earned, it was time for me to pivot away. I had allowed myself to be swallowed by it all and eventually found the frustration overbearing. It was all perfect harmony outside of the fact that I could have chosen to leave about six months sooner.

Checking in with your body daily and using the tools we will be learning together here will keep you present and in momentum, instead of losing months of precious time, like I did. I was sitting in a roller coaster of chaos and frustration. Can you relate? I'm sure you've been there, but hopefully not for months.

At the beginning of working with the company, everything felt expansive; towards the end, it was a constrictive experience. Metaphorically, it was choking me alive, and I sensed it. Yes, my body was talking to me! Interestingly enough, I traded a coaching session with an exceptional healer, now a friend of mine, Alex Mei, who at the time knew nothing about where I worked during our first session together. He asked about my job, sensing it was a vampire sucking my blood out. I gave my resignation notice within weeks of this appointment. The point is: start noticing what you're experiencing within your body as you're taking in every moment of your day.

How are you doing?

Is what you're up to every day making your body feel light and joyful about life?

I'm now back to allowing my body to guide me, it appears that I had taken a two-year hiatus-I didn't. I was only listening to the details that I was willing to grasp at that moment. Selective listening! I wasn't paying attention to the overarching veil of weight that was lying on top of me, bringing me down.

Friends were there for me, listening to my frustrations. I have always known that when I'm frustrated, digging my heels into the ground, I get to shift! My friends and clients always ask me what my gut says. Usually, I rhetorically ask them the same thing. *What does your body say?*

When I feel frustrated or have what feels like a bad day, I know there is a lesson to learn or a shift to make. Bad days illuminate the deeper spaces we can delve into. Learn about what's creating the situation and then change to a new experience. You can also ignore bad feelings, knowing tomorrow is a better day if you choose. Yet, the situation may repeat itself soon. There's no need to get mad at bad days. Simply step into the NOW. Become inquisitive and let the guidance unfold.

Get ready for new days and ways of being by launching into a space of curiosity. Leave the disgust in the dust. You are at the beginning of a bold journey towards body enlightenment.

First, let's dive into clearing the chaos and dirt so that you may be reborn, with a new foundation. Then, you'll learn to allow your body to lead the way. Give it a voice. It's ready in the NOW. Let's move the dust from your light so you may shine with the wisdom of trees and their wondrous beauty.

In your current life, is there a situation that makes you feel icky inside?

WEEK ONE - EARTH
ONE'S FOUNDATION

Being in tune with ourselves and finding alignment requires an in-depth awareness of self and of what becoming aware means. Ultimately, you can be your own life coach when you use the tools presented in this book. For starters, creating awareness comes from presence. This first week you will start with a blank slate and learn to build a strong foundation to a thriving new mindset.

Think of the earth that the tree digs deep roots into. If the ground is unstable, you'll find yourself with a falling tree as soon as there is a flash flood or windstorm. When the dirt is unhealthy, not receiving vital nutrients or water, you may end up with a dead tree, an infestation, or a tree that doesn't have enough power and immunity to ward off disease. Similarly, when you create your healthy and stable roots, from home life to work life, you'll be firm in all your daily choices. In this chapter, we want to set up your foundation so that you are firm in everything you are, do, and have.

This understanding of a stable context from which you operate will strengthen your intuition and create a connection to your self, your surroundings, and others. How you do one thing is how you do everything. It's crucial to start your journey in the right place. A fresh start needs a clean foundation to bring clarity and re-focused energy into the space.

Becoming in touch with ourselves starts with a commitment to being more observant and intentional every single day. Throughout the upcoming weeks, we will build upon new levels of dedication and skills that are necessary to reap the benefits of a present and conscious lifestyle. I'm committed to helping you hone your internal compass and own the answers received within. It's an honor to walk through the journey alongside my clients and friends, now doing the same with you. It is important to me that you know the truth because once you understand it, freedom is certain. This is especially true for over-analyzers who have analysis paralysis, need suggestions from everyone else and require lots of research and time before making decisions – they are going to experience incredible freedom through understanding body intelligence!

The next few weeks will equip you to build a deeper trust within yourself so that you can act out confidently, without hesitation. You will gain a deeper understanding of which situations create specific goals in your personal and professional life. This journey is about discovering what tools, skills, and resources are available within yourself for you to develop a personalized process that honors your motivations – and ultimately manifests them.

There are infinite possibilities for our intuitive nature. People all over the world, from different backgrounds (including myself), have experienced the fantastic results of alignment and the guidance that stem from tapping into this internal power. The beauty and wonder of a more profound intuition can provide an alignment with life, which is magical.

Yes, I mention "magic" - don't throw away the book just yet! Magic, by my definition, is achieving indescribable results, similar to miracles, from the power of focusing our aligned energy. Since energy is discussed throughout the book, before we go any further, my view and definition of energy needs addressing.

Energy breaks down to all the molecules and atoms that make up the earth. There is a push and pull, a negative and positive attraction - like that of magnets - through which units respond to each other. Molecules bounce off of each other and move, vibrating throughout the Universe in either unison or opposition. Molecules can work in harmony and balance. The result is chaos when they do not. The 1977 version of the short film *Powers of Ten*, by co-creators Charles & Ray Eames, addresses the differences and similarities between the macro and the micro: the Universe and human cells. They look the same. Pretty magical, right?

Plants, animals, inanimate objects, everything and everyone is made up of atoms and molecules that are responding to each other. Nothing is solid. Once you have grasped the knowledge that there isn't any distinction between anything or anyone, based on science (quantum physics in particular), you start to recognize how easy it is to influence the energy within you, your environment, and space.

Two other terms commonly used throughout this book are 'higher vibrations' and 'frequencies'. When we are at a higher level of vibration/frequency, we enter into a space of harmony or alignment in our life. The highest vibrational space brings about our goals and aspirations, with ease. Also, in this space, hurdles and challenges are more naturally accepted and easier to overcome.

Starting with a strong foundation takes focus. Every step from here on out will need your attention and commitment to work. It's important to remember this and keep your goals in mind as motivation for when the desire for instant gratification starts to show.

Multiple reasons are motivating each of us to find alignment and expand our awareness through intuitive connection with ourselves and our surroundings. It's important to remember that we all start from the same place: atoms and molecules, attracting and opposing. Your ground zero might be below sea level right now, or it could be on top of the Himalayas. It's time to set a clear space – both mentally and physically.

Clearing builds the strong foundation that you will need throughout the coming weeks. You will soon recognize how everything is related. The initial time for space clearing will take some dedication at first. Feel free to bring your friends along on this ride, for added accountability. Together you can succeed in this process.

Whether you are achieving great success or struggling to find your breakthrough – clearing your space is the most fundamental skill that will allow you to master presence. A space clearing strategy isn't a one-time event in building a stronger intuition. You may find yourself coming back to this step many times.

Action Plans for Each Week:

When you feel complete, you will be ready for the next week of exercises. Keep in mind that weekly practices don't have to happen consecutively. You can take an extra week if you need more time or revisit any of the days, for as long as you need, in a way that works best for you.

If, for any reason, you don't feel that this coincides with your Being, make an inventory of what you may have missed or refused to do. Do not delay in making these corrections! This awareness will support you in understanding possible gaps in your life and places where you may need to do a little more digging to understand why you're not willing to move forward. This will support you later in figuring out why you aren't where you want to be. You chose this book for a reason, right? You've got this!

Day One: Countering a Culture of Distractions

The average adult in North America has a shorter attention span (8 seconds) than a goldfish (9 seconds). That is 4 seconds slower than the tested attention span in 2000[1].

In a culture of multitaskers, social media notifications, and addictive Netflix & HBO series, it's easy to see why accomplishing our goals can feel like a chore. There are always a million advertising messages coming at us from every direction! These messages often make us feel hopeless. They most definitely are not about our ability to use internal power to better ourselves. Your true capabilities begin by separating your inner dialogue from the noise of external messages.

Right now, your inner dialogue is probably similar to talking on a mobile phone with an overly protective case muffling your voice. Your case might give you security about protecting your phone, but what good is it if you can't use it correctly? It's crucial to not succumb to the false sense of security that distractions can provide.

The most common distraction people currently have is their mobile phone. Whether you are team Apple or Android doesn't matter. The fact that those teams exist at all proves that they affect how we interact with the world. – and how we see ourselves. Yes, they keep us in touch with loved ones and up to

---

[1] The study can be found at: http://www.telegraph.co.uk/science/2016/03/12/humans-have-shorter-attention-span-than-goldfish-thanks-to-smart/

date on information. However, they also fill those uncomfortable voids that are screaming to be noticed.

The average person's inability to handle moments of silence is filled by swiping on social media and news. Try not to look at your phone or listen to music the next time you are taking an Uber or Lyft, walking to the store, or waiting for an appointment. It's ok to admit that the unoccupied mental space makes you feel uneasy. Be honest with yourself and know that being distracted doesn't mean anything more about your character; you are merely human. On the bright side, more and more people are deleting these apps from their phones as they recognize they have become addictions.

Throughout the day, a great way to identify distractions is writing down your shifts of focus as they come to mind. They could be notifications on your phone, random thoughts about someone in your life, or even something that appears productive – like checking on work emails while you're off the clock. My notifications for apps are now entirely off, outside of phone calls.

There's a fine line between multi-tasking and being distracted. They can both prevent you from hearing what your body is trying to tell you. One of the best ways to tell the difference is by asking yourself if something is crucial before doing it. It might be even more helpful to gauge the need on a scale of one to five - one being non-threatening and five being "Holy Smokes!" and writing down the number next to your task when you're tracking them throughout the day. By using a small, even-numbered scale, you are creating a more intentional priority system, which can carry into the decision-making throughout your intuitive journey. Anything that falls into the 1 or 2 categories is most likely a distraction.

Developing this system also increases the skill of discernment – the ability to perceive without judgment. The skills are extremely important in developing a stronger connection within. Properly prioritizing our distractions also helps to cut the ultimate distraction of "indifference" by not giving yourself a middle-ground option.

Part of strengthening our body's guidance means being honest with ourselves. We must not make excuses to avoid listening to our thoughts. Accepting distracting behaviors from yourself or others is a defense mechanism to bypass vulnerability. Part of building a stronger foundation means we get comfortable being honest and open. Recognizing distractions and excuses will highlight personal faults within yourself. It's vital to not beat yourself up about it and continue to work through challenges.

Issues like social anxiety and other similar conditions are very legitimate variables that you should keep in mind. You should be in the right place to understand the triggers for self-destructive behaviors and other mental health issues that might make this process more difficult. Seek professional guidance as you work through this process. Know that it is possible to overcome these variables as you work towards a clearer path. Use this tool throughout your journey of healing.

Be aware of which distractions feel the most ordinary to you. Start with what's familiar, and you'll be prepared to recognize the more subtle ones as you progress throughout this alignment trek. Make peace with the fact that this will take time. The diligence is well worth it.

Days Two-Three: Mastering Your Environment

Understanding the connection between our physical environments and our mental clarity makes a difference in creating a more harmonious life. The average North American person sees more than 5000 advertisements a day[2]. While this might feel overwhelming, you are more in control than you realize.

We have become so accustomed to being distracted that we've made it our norm, along with feeling overwhelmed and hopeless, or always trying to keep up. It might seem like you can never truly get away from the noise of responsibility or your phone. However, making a committed effort can make a grand difference in strengthening your inner voice.

In writing this book, I have had to find places with zero distractions, turned my phone off, as well as shut down any notifications and alerts on my computer. Every little beep could quickly draw me to something else, and next thing you know, nothing would get done.

---

[2] According to a study from 2006, by Walker Smith.

Rob Bell is a phenomenal speaker and author who gets creative about being intentional. I was invited to attend one of his talks and he shared a perspective on how our environment can affect our creative process.

Bell asked us to envision ourselves sitting inside the walls of a Walgreens or CVS pharmacy store and try to get creative ideas flowing. Next, he asked us to see ourselves sitting in the Sistine Chapel, captivated by the sacred details of this artistic masterpiece.

"Where do you feel you would be most inspired, at ease, and allowing for the creativity to flow through you?" Bell asked us rhetorically.

Weigh the difference of your creative output when sitting at a flimsy card table on a cheap folding chair versus a chair that is a piece of art, or even a comfortable chaise lounge. These minute differences present some of the first barriers to your creative success. People don't always seem to understand the impact that their external environments have on daily decisions and interests. Being in an environment that calms the mind is essential to getting in tune with your internal guidance.

Imagine meditating or praying within that Walgreens versus the Sistine Chapel. Yes, it technically can be done in either place, however, which is going to be the more accessible place to go deep in flow with your experience?

The most natural place to start is the most controllable space we inhabit – our homes. How does your home make you feel?

Tap into the consciousness of what your body feels when you walk in. As you enter your home, take a moment to close your eyes, listen, and observe your experience. Start listening to your body and the guidance it is sharing with you.

If your home is cluttered, then that's the first place to start. Clutter is distracting because, in the back of our mind, our brain is stressing about the fact that things need to be cleaned up, which takes up necessary brainpower. From the moment you enter your home, this chaos trickles in and affects it both personally and professionally.

A fellow life coach once told me that he wouldn't consult with clients unless their bedroom was clean. If someone calls him with a burning situation, his first words are "What does your bedroom look like right now?" If it's not clean and organized, he tells them to call him back when it is. Guess what? 95% of the time, they don't call him back because, by the time they have organized their room, the situation that they were calling about had been handled. The two go hand in hand proving that how we do one thing is how we do everything.

Day Four: Feng Shui

Let's start with taking physical control of your home, and then you can decide which of the proposed methods might work for your other personal spaces. Let's get the positive energy flowing!

I'm a big proponent of Feng Shui (pronounced "fung shway"), the ancient Chinese practice of working with your environment, intentions, shifting things around, and activating harmony with your life-force energy, or Chi.

My enthusiasm for Feng Shui started over a decade ago. I was in charge of finding home buyers to fill an entirely new condominium complex. Selling the first unit, that very first bite, seemed to take forever. Getting creative, I called in a Feng Shui consultant who gave me all kinds of minor adjustment suggestions.

Before I had even completed all of my Feng Shui tasks, I received a full price offer within 12 hours. That moment was magical to me. I still commit to these practices and rituals often. It's all about intention, which brings about aligned results.

I started to have my Feng Shui consultant come to every home I was selling, as well as to my own home. She also assisted me in creating a harmonious vibe through energy shifts at my office, on marketing materials, and even in my car!

Feng Shui is now a part of my daily life. You will rarely find my home a mess, or even my toilet seats up, as in Feng Shui, this represents money and opportunities flushing down the drain. Organization and cleanliness are fundamental. The last thing I want is disorder or confusion brought into my life from things that I could have easily changed.

Feng Shui is more than rearranging furniture and performing rituals. Above all else, it is a foundation for focusing your attention on specific details within your life and taking action to change them. Consider it similar to the concept of the "Law of Attraction", coined by Madame Blavatsky, over a century ago. Feng Shui helps us establish the intention to attract what we want and detract from what we don't. Remember, everything is connected.

There are many specific guidelines to Feng Shui; however, you don't want to stress over the specifics. I'm sharing with you the ones that I find most impactful in clearing space in order to build a deeper connection with your intuition and ultimately getting you aligned in your life. Surrounding yourself with a clean environment results in a clear and present mind, which is necessary when being in-tune with your body intelligence.

The Bedroom:

It all starts with a few simple questions for when you enter your bedroom.

Is it clean and organized?

Does it look like an inviting place for you to walk into and relax?

Is your mind racing with things to do?

These are probably the most straightforward questions to answer, especially if the answer is no. If you are busy or lean towards a procrastinating nature, it will be very tempting to try to find a yes in your response where it shouldn't be. Take this as a practice in honesty. Don't let yourself cut corners here.

Start cleaning and organizing, even if it's just a little at a time. Get those sheets washed. Put away everything that is not bringing peace and love into your being and space - or remove altogether.

If your place isn't that messy, but you still feel it's stagnant, move every single piece of furniture around, even if it's only a couple of inches. The intention is to move the energy in the room. The slightest change can create inspiration, reveal something that might be hidden or awaken a message within.

Do not have any mirrors facing your bed. They reflect energy back at you instead of dispersing it, which can cause difficulty sleeping.

Similarly, if there is a fan above your bed, try your best not to have it on while you sleep, or you will have your body's energy field churning in circles all night long as a result.

Remove electronics from your room, even TV's, or have alarm clocks face away from you. Include your cell phones! Have your phone in airplane mode to keep radiation at bay, also remove blue light. Blue light can prevent your body's production of melatonin, the natural hormone that provides rejuvenating sleep.

Don't bring work into your bedroom, as it can keep your mind in work mode, especially when sleeping. Do you have pictures on your bedroom walls of anyone – or anything - that stresses you out? Remove them. Also, if you're seeking romance, clear out pictures of family and children.

Once you feel peace and relaxation as you enter your room, you will also feel revitalized when you wake up. Your sleep is not only vital to your health, it is also essential to your cortisol levels. Cortisol supports your emotions and ability to remain calm, amongst many other health benefits. Sleep affects your ability to be present and aware of guidance from your body.

The Home:

Now that you are sleeping better, feeling energized, and hopefully excited about your bedroom, let's discuss the rest of your home. First off, even if you are broke and living off of your sister's couch, wherever you lay your head at night is home, so you get to own it. Feel empowered to hold your space – no matter how small or temporary it might be - and gain strength from the changes.

Now that you know where home is, let's make the space inviting, warm, and cozy. You deserve it.

Cleaning and organization are essential, from head-to-toe, ceiling-to-floor. If you want to hire a deep cleaner, go for it. Make sure you are also involved because this is also an energetic personal cleaning. Be in the experience of bringing love into your home, as you clean up, organize, and get those fixes made that keep showing up on the end of your to-do list.

Continue placing the intention of clearing out the negative energy that doesn't serve you. Holding this in your mind invites harmony into your home and is an excellent practice for improving focus.

If you can accomplish this one task you are one huge step ahead. Think of how much better it will feel in your newly organized space!

Take this opportunity to move furniture around so that the space feels open and welcoming. Listen to your body and your heart as you make these shifts. See if you can start to hear anything within yourself. Even if you are only moving the furniture an inch, the energy moves because we are shifting it. Ultimately the shifts support opening awareness to allow a path towards guidance.

Have you heard of the popular Netflix show *Tidying Up* with Marie Kondo? Her approach is very pertinent and valuable, and it also speaks in terms of body intelligence. If an item doesn't spark joy within you, she says, it's time to thank it and pass it along to someone who will be happy to use it.

Day Five: Minimalism

Adapting the practice of minimalism, getting rid of excess, helps us stay clear. *If you don't need it, wear it, or use it – then it's time to get rid of it.* Clear out that closet, do that spring cleaning, get the garage organized, bring those boxes of things to someone who would use them.

If you have a habit of hoarding everything you get, try changing your perspective to the present. You are on your way towards a new experience and sometimes that can mean new stuff as well. You'll need somewhere to put it, right?

Maybe you're planning on being more productive and profitable. If you bring the minimalist practice to your work, you may find yourself more prosperous – it could also lead to you finally finding a forever home, as all is intertwined. If you're planning to move in the next few years, shed what you don't need. Plan for it now, why wait? According to Feng Shui practices, these small intentional actions could be the push needed to create what I like to call aligned results.

The hardest part is getting rid of things that you've developed an emotional attachment to. However, once you do release them, you will rarely look back and regret it. When we rid ourselves of the "old," we are opening ourselves to the "new". This task might take a little longer than a week to do. If the intention is there and you are in constant action, the results will flourish.

Day Six: Attention to Detail

Clearing up your space can be an emotional process, but it is necessary for the intention of bringing only good and well being from here on out. I pray you are getting the point here. Don't take these matters lightly. I have heard of people cleaning their home and placing bubbling fountains in specific places to then receive raises from their jobs the very next day. Clearing and moving items around support your goals when using distinct intention.

Let's move into the details: how's your wallet, is it full of old receipts? Empty it. When you are cleaning out your space, remember you are making room for those additional dollars and new income checks.

Address the clutter in every physical way that you can. It will not only clear your physical space, it frees mental capacity as well for supporting your mindfulness. Remember, your home is a reflection of your life. Do your best to stay focused during this process.

Wash the car, vacuum it, clear out stagnant energy and invite the harmonious power of safety and love as you travel. Every little bit adds up. Self-care builds love and security. When you feel more secure, you will act with confidence and will see the ripple effects of these small actions showing up from your daily intentions.

Don't forget to take the time to clean up your technology devices too! If you are like me, you are using them daily, and it's affecting your life dramatically. Delete unnecessary emails and files. It is vital to create openness in your space. Bringing in the new energy, we are going to tap into the flow of new opportunities, and also to get rid of the nagging distractions that keep you from living the life of your dreams. It's time to stop swatting at life's "bugs" and enjoy the space you're in.

My experience as a real estate agent has shown this to me multiple times. It's a huge transition to move, let alone buy and sell a property that you were maybe not planning on selling for a much longer time. However, sometimes, people are ready to change things up. Our physical spaces are a great representation of this change of energy.

Here is a personal example: my friend Laura told me one day that she and her husband had decided to sell their new home. I was utterly shocked at this decision because it was a beautiful and spacious home. They were planning to move to another house that was not necessarily different, or in a better location. My experience of Laura's home was warm and cozy, yet to her, it brought anger as soon as she walked in the door. Not good! It is also important to note the events that have previously taken place in your home, or during past occupancies. That energy lingers in your space even after you bring your own energy into it. This is another reason I practice Feng Shui with real estate listings and do blessings for clients.

Laura's home was brand new, so past occupants' energy couldn't have been the cause. There could have been negative energy related to the land, possibly conflicts involving developers of previous landowners. For Laura, this home had negative energy because of her familial situation, fights with her husband, and the constant, overwhelming pressure of keeping the home tidy while raising young children.

As a life coach and practitioner of Feng Shui, I would encourage someone in Laura's situation to go through the process described in week 1 to create a new environment within her home and note if anything changes, before deciding to sell. Simple changes might shift the energy up and avoid the headaches and added stress of moving to another house, while bringing harmony and coziness within those same walls.

Sometimes moving the energy and clearing things out will not give you the blank slate you desire. To truly get a home cleared out, additional blessings and clearing can be used to get a fresh start.

Day Seven: Clearing Your Space

Now that you have cleaned and re-organized your home and refreshed the space, it's time to empty it of those last remnants of negative and stale energy, through the mighty cleansing power of sage or other tools.

Saging space for clearing is a Native American ritual. Similar practices can be found in many forms amongst various religions and spiritual practices.

For instance, in Feng Shui, the clearing practice involves breaking up the stagnant energy with sound. The Chinese use unique metal bells and chimes to clamor, to create change through sound vibration. You can also use your hands and clap loudly. If you are looking for a fun experience, you want to be with me on Chinese New Year's Eve. I even have family and friends now bringing some of these practices into their own home after a Chinese New Years' Eve gathering. The positive energy from banging pots and pans in every nook and corner, behind doors, and opening all the windows in the freezing weather and throwing orange peels everywhere provides an incredibly euphoric feeling that empowers you to take ownership of the energy in your space.

Many people use sage regularly. Sage not only removes the negative energy and spirits, but it also lifts good energy and good spirits. So when you are "saging" your belongings and spaces, it's relevant to replace the negative energy with the positive energy and affirmations of your choice.

First, grab your chosen tool for ridding negative spirits - maybe sage, palo santo wood sticks- best gotten from a Shaman as these are endangered trees, bells, or metal pots - and have them ready for action. Then open your windows and turn on ALL the lights. Take your tool of choice and use it throughout your home, behind doors, in the closets, corners, around windows, above your bed, and break up that energy, getting out every last bit of negativity and staleness. As you go around breaking it all up, envision the windows pulling out all that doesn't serve you, like a vacuum transmuting it for good by Mother Earth or Gaia.

Now you have fragmented energy in your space. Go through your home again with the burning incense of your choice. Push out the broken-up energy and invite the goodness in. The Chinese often burn the incense of Chen Pi or dried mandarin orange peels. Tibetans also use incense, and so do Christian churches. Sandalwood is great for general well-being and goodness. You can also find various Tibetan herbal medicine incense that could include prayer intentions. There are many other choices as well; it all comes down to getting intentional and harnessing the benefits specific to your chosen incense. It doesn't matter what you use, as long as it works and feels right for you.

No negativity should be affecting your decisions, at home or elsewhere. When you are at your home, you want to feel in control in a safe and loving environment.

The windows and lights should still be open. You can also light candles. I have a red and white candle pair that I use for my energy work. White candles are powerful and symbolize truth. Also, white includes all the colors. Focus on your intention through every step of this process. As I light my candles, I say out loud "Only surround me with the highest and purest light."

Take your incense and walk through your home, through every nook and cranny, behind doors, closets, and curtains. As you walk through the place, set an intention. Repeat an affirmation or mantra to stay focused.

Let's take my friend Laura's example, who has had too many arguments with her husband and financial stress. If I were her, I'd be walking around my home with the incense while continually saying out loud " I release the old and bring love, harmony, and prosperity into my home." Figure out what statement feels best to you. I would say this again and again, walking throughout the entire home with the incense. The incense carries what doesn't serve you out through the windows, and holds on to the goodness that you are creating inside.

When you have finished the incense and blessings ritual, you can close the windows and turn off the lights. Light stands for the highest, most positive energy. Lamps and candles shed light on the negative energies, pushing them out the windows. The process is similar to that of incense.

Once we reach a comfortable place with our home, we get a stronger sense of belonging, of being "grounded". Shooting for the stars takes a lot of will-power. However, the journey seems a lot less scary when we know there is a safe place to land.

How are you feeling in your home now? Is it a peaceful haven? Feel free to turn up the music, sing, dance, celebrate, have a fantastic meal or a decadent dessert. Keep bringing in the love and joy to your space, and these actions will cement it. Maybe you have a party! At this point, your home should feel amazing, comfortable, and be bringing you so much joy! The foundation you build during this week will create the long-lasting results that you are looking for.

SUMMARY - EARTH

Day 1: Countering a Culture of Distractions
- Discover what is distracting you from listening to yourself and being more intentional in your life.
- Create a list of daily distractions and rate them on a scale.

Days 2-3: Mastering Your Environment
- Assess which environments affect your energy, and note how they do it.
- Determine which atmospheres (physical or mental) affect your state of peace the most.

Day 4: Feng Shui
- Take notice of how your bedroom feels.
- Determine what to remove from the space that is not serving your harmony and quality of sleep.

Day 5: Minimalism
- Physically rid your home of unnecessary objects that may bring negative or stagnant energy.

Day 6: Attention to Detail
- Rearrange your space to create a positive environment that instills peace and rest.

Day 7: Clearing Your Space
• Do the spiritual cleansing of your choice.

Try leaving for a day or two after finishing the cleansing practices and see how different your home feels after you return, now that it is clean and organized.

Tip: If you feel it isn't necessary to cleanse your home before you get it organized, make sure you do a cleansing ritual after you've finished organizing it.

You can apply this process to your car, office, etc. In my work, I often deal with businesses, clearing stagnant energy when something is shifting - for example, an organizational change. I also consult clients who are selling their homes or moving into a new one. I encourage you to bring others into the process - your family, your partner, employees, or an amazing friend. Having multiple people support you and your vision magnifies the magnetic attraction of it.

This cleansing and blessing can be done weekly or monthly as a practice in setting an intention for the new and clearing out the old. I recommend doing it at least once a season, to reflect seasonal changes and the shift in nature's energy and during any notable life changes like new jobs, positions, relationships, and breakups.

What has shifted the most after clearing your foundation?

WEEK TWO - ROOTS
CLEARING SELF

Your roots, like those of a tree, are the starting point of your information intake, and create contact with others. Trees communicate through their network of underground roots, which reach far and wide. In receiving and perceiving incoming information with your body, you want to have a clear mind and body. Every moment you are communicating with the world, projecting outwards.

This week, we want to create a free space for you to listen and receive, so that when you communicate, it is an unsoiled transmission coming from a pure space.

Clearing and cleansing create an openness of space for new information, new relationships and new opportunities to come in, as we learn to listen to our bodies. Now that the external purging and groundwork are complete, we must clear the internal space as well. Cleansing will align you with your goals and desires, through inner dialogue, guidance, and strength.

Inner strength brings about equanimity - mental and emotional neutrality - which ensures that emotions do not swing violently throughout daily challenges. One way of attaining equanimity is working through 'unfinished business' with family, friends, work colleagues and past relationships. There could be emotional ties, forgiveness, or debts needing attention as well.

Taking responsibility for past and current situations, while mentally letting go, is essential. One starts tapping into full-body experiences by feeling into emotions, chakras, or energy fields, and clearing out any last bits of lingering negative energy.

This chapter will introduce inner clearings; by the end of it, you will find that there is so much light behind the veils you've removed. The deeper dive you take with your efforts, the bigger the rewards. Remember, how you do one thing is how you do everything.

Day One: Commit to a Clear Mind

Listening to your internal compass is more than a goal – it's a commitment to balance: a state where you feel in control of your life, and fully accept that you are not in control of your life, simultaneously. It's a state of peace that is uniquely harmonious to your body and soul's needs.

Your body and soul's needs describe your personal nature, which is the biggest motivator for your actions - actions you are both aware and unaware of. A large part of that balance comes from being true to your nature, while also being open to change, when necessary. Throughout the next weeks, there will be more in-depth discussions of getting in touch with your view and attaining the stillness of balance. However, before we can grasp stillness and listen to the messages, we must understand what balance means for our minds.

When you're balanced, your mind is in a mentally clear state that ignores distractions and stays focused on tasks. As I'm re-reading this particular page, I'm thoroughly distracted and noticing myself pulled in multiple directions. Reading this line brought a smile to my face, making me take a moment to pause and refocus. Building this clarity is a practice that will help you succeed in the body intelligence-driven lifestyle. It's something you will continuously strive towards, and it becomes easier to find as you develop your awareness of body intelligence.

It might sound like a rerun of past New Year resolutions, yet being consciously intentional can quickly become habitual when we see the immediate benefits it brings into our lives. Most of the time, we don't realize how our daily distractions affect what should be our most memorable experiences, until it's too late.

Over a decade ago, I had the opportunity to go to Thailand for almost a month. Out of all the things I could have been thinking about during that trip, beyond the exotic culture and breathtaking sites – sitting in the back of my mind was this nagging anxiety about finding wi-fi so I could keep up with work, family, and friends. Looking back, I'm kind of disappointed with myself! Experiencing every moment without a single distraction is difficult for even the most dedicated person.

The great thing about this part of the journey is the endless opportunity to practice getting it right. Giving ourselves little victories every day can make clarity a natural process, but first, we've got to be aware of them.

A friend of mine, Krista Petty, facilitates experiential learning environments for personal growth. Not only does she help her clients build essential skills, she's a prime example of what committing to intentional living can do for your quality of life. I commend Krista for being a leadership success, balancing her trainings around the world, and living her personal life! For the longest time, I didn't understand how she was able to get so much from her days. When she isn't traveling around the world leading workshops or being a business CEO, somehow, she still has time to enjoy her family, during her children's most crucial years.

After she assured me that she was genuinely happy wearing many hats, I asked her for her secret sauce, and I'll never forget what she told me:

"When I choose to teach a workshop, meet a friend for lunch, or go to an event, as long as I know that I will be 100% fully present, I'll choose to attend."

It was such a simple answer, and a light bulb went off in my head. I was surprised and speechless. Krista lives in the moment as much as she can. The commitment radiates positive energy that not only benefits her life, it also affects all those touched by her. That's when I realized the beauty we can allow ourselves to have – even while busy – through committing to being intentional with our interactions.

Think about it - How does your life compare to this situation?

Baby steps. In my case, I start small, doing everything I can to keep my phone distractions at bay and out of my hands when I'm with people. If I'm out with a friend at lunch, I won't check my phone while they talk. As soon as the person goes to the restroom, though, I may reach into my handbag to look at my phone. Sometimes I'll challenge myself and not allow that either, as even the little act of glimpsing at my phone screen could quickly set my mind racing.

If this doesn't resonate with you, I want to take a moment to acknowledge you for your dedication to being present with your friends and family. Be honest with yourself and ask your friends to make sure you're not doing this unconsciously, in "automatic mode." If you truly are present when you are with others, it's people like you and Krista who inspire a better future for us all!

Day Two: Taking Responsibility

Today is a big day! It's time to take responsibility. Many people like to play the victim of circumstances in their life, but that is a disempowering place to live from.

When I moved to Los Angeles, I dove straight into work. Work, work, work. Now, because I "chose" (responsible keyword) to focus on my career instead of my love life, the last thing I could do is complain about not meeting any men. Had I moved to Los Angeles with the intent of being in a relationship, I would have immediately hopped on dating apps, joined meet up groups, and gone out intentionally to meet men. However, this was not the choice I had made. That is why, two years after my move to Los Angeles, I had no right to gripe about not finding a match. Additionally, there was no room to complain about the fact that even though I lived right on the beach, right on the boardwalk, I hadn't even attempted surfing. I had a moment of frustration when I came to this realization. I had not taken the opportunity to try surfing when I was living on the beach; instead, I had been cooped up in my place, working, day after day, on a company I ended up shutting down anyways.

Instead of living with regret, I took notice and made an inventory of what I wanted to change in my life at that point. I then took responsibility for being in a relationship, created action, and eventually met an amazing man.

Here's another example, generic yet commonly played out: someone gets laid off from work. They whine and moan that their boss is awful, and act as a victim of the firing. Then they look back at the previous couple of months and realize that whining and moaning about the lost position was a waste of time and step into a conscious understanding of what they could have done differently. They take responsibility for being laid off.

I call this situation "sourcing" because the individual "sourced" the layoff. When they take the time to reminisce, they might remember all the times they had had an inner dialogue wishing for a different job, or working with someone else. Sourcing is where the Universe conspires to get them exactly what they thought about most. They drew it in with their thoughts.

The same principle applied when I got divorced. My memory is of my ex-husband walking downstairs one morning to make his coffee, before taking off to work and casually stating he was "done" as he poured his coffee into a coffee mug. I was entirely baffled by this random comment, and it took me twenty more minutes to understand that he was stating he wanted a divorce. In those first moments, I felt ambushed wholly by the information. It came out of the blue! Yet did it?

Later that year, as I was taking a trip to Europe, I started reading my journal while sitting in the Paris airport for a long layover. I had never actually read my journal before. During that period of my life, I was only using my journal for brain dumping, when things were frustrating, in trying to pump myself back up (you'll find that I use it for much more, nowadays). As I read through pages of what seemed like infinite awful incidents between my ex and myself, I was in disbelief of how often I had poured out onto the pages, stating I wanted to break up and get a divorce! It was crazy! I couldn't recollect these thoughts intentionally, yet through sub-consciousness writing, apparently, that's what I had wanted. Also, that journal only recorded negative experiences, covering quite a few years of our relationship.

Looking back, I can clearly see that I had been unconsciously asking to break up and get divorced from this guy for quite some time. He certainly wasn't the right match for a stable relationship. Even though I wasn't fully aware of my desires, the Universe heard my subconscious wishes. Therefore I had "sourced it", I had sourced my divorce. From a fully responsible place, I chose into the divorce. The thoughts I had been having for a while brought about the demise of the relationship, although I didn't recognize them until reading through my journal.

Sourcing is another form of responsibility. When you source something, it means that you had a powerful thought, whether negative or positive, that brought about a circumstance into your life. Sourcing is one of the most impactful things affecting our lives, and we must truly understand it. In principle, we are responsible for what we create in our life. We manifest, according to the law of attraction.

Let's consider a negative situation where it would be easy to be a victim. One of my close girlfriends tends to source a lot of adverse events in her life, from car accidents and people stealing money from her to the craziest traumatic dates, to name a few.

People who wreak havoc generally have some chaotic energy that they've either created in this life or has been with them for lifetimes.

Well, this friend of mine has some energy that's out of alignment, even though she is also a very aware person. She knows how to take responsibility because she's emotionally intelligent. Regardless, she hasn't done the work to clear the negative energy of childhood experiences, so they keep playing out through drama and traumatic situations.

Do you or does a friend have lots of reoccurring drama? These trends are necessary to address. You will learn how to tackle them as you read through the next chapters.

When we think about something we want to manifest, it's imperative to start from a clean, positive, and happy place. Should I look for a boyfriend because I was alone and sad, then most likely, the guys that I would end up dating would mirror that troubled state. However, since I was looking for a match, someone who was loving, joyful, and supportive, I found someone who truly embodies the qualities I wanted to manifest in a partner.

This thought process is essentially a twist to the conventional ways of thinking because it's about taking ownership of the situation created by our thoughts and actions. One of the workshops I have designed is called 'From Fear to Freedom by Owning Your Story'. During one transformative night of teaching this workshop, I witnessed the weight drop off of people's shoulders, as they vulnerably shared situations they felt victims of. For some people, getting to the point of being able to voice them out loud was a remarkable process in itself. As others shared their stories, it supported those less inclined to do so. When they shared a 'story', it no longer owned them, there was a lightness to it. Based on this experience, I have created the anthology 'Owning Our Stories' as a platform for people to let their stories get out, break free, release, and let it all go.

Before going through an emotional intelligence course, I had been seeing a physical therapist for piriformis issues that would leave my legs numb during specific workouts. My physical therapist would note how tight I was from my hips to my abs, as she'd painfully dig deep underneath my rib cage to do some muscle release work. After two weeks of emotional courses, including lots of cathartic work, she noticed that my abs were quite loose, and I had let go. The physical therapist wanted to know what I had done. Our bodies, feelings, thoughts, and stories are entirely intertwined. It is possible to have physical ailments within our body and muscle fibers disappear through new understandings and acknowledgement of past situations that produced stored emotions. I let go of painful situations during the workshops which then allowed my abs to loosen up thus creating a ripple effect to also support my hips and piriformis issues.

For today's exercise, I encourage you to let all the negative situations, past and present, surface. Find a way to take ownership of them; it is only a mental shift. You can take ownership, by vocalizing them, writing them out or sharing with someone you trust. You can take responsibility by recognizing past thoughts that might have triggered current situations.

When you recognize situations from a place of "What did I do to source and create this?" you can clear away negative thought patterns through awareness. The new considerations will open you up to alignment and to creating with intention everything that you want to attract into your life, moving forward.

Considering these questions can be a challenging process in some situations, so maybe pass over some experiences and think about others. For traumatic experiences, talking to someone who specializes in trauma could supply valuable insight. Some situations may have been past down from past lives and familial lineage, so they will require more complex and sustained consideration.

Know that regardless of what has happened, you deserve a shift for the best. At the same time, understanding your thought processes might illuminate certain situations in your life that will require your attention more than others. Maybe you have old journals to read through as well? They could provide useful windows into your soul's deepest desires and thoughts.

Day Three: Equanimity

Now that you know how to take responsibility, we can continue neutralizing situations by learning to resolve and clear them. Taking responsibility for your actions will support you in your relationships. Wouldn't it be nice to have a community that is a drama-free zone? Think of how much more fun and joyous you can be with your friends when there is no drama. Well, you have the opportunity to be the first in neutralizing and creating that drama-free community.

I used to live with one of my friends, whom I adore. Even though we had an absolute blast together, I knew that if either one of us was going to have momentum with what we were creating, we needed to be living in separate places. Eventually, we got to the point where I was going to move out, or she needed to; I had reached my tipping point and needed to "put on my oxygen mask first".

The conversation felt heavy; we both cried, yet, in the end, there was only beauty. We both knew in our hearts that it was the right decision. I'm sure you can relate to similar situations where you care about someone so deeply and don't want to hurt them. Yet, you know that a conversation needs to happen because otherwise, you would be living with the heaviness of not taking action.

Here are four steps to take for this type of conversation to yield a positive outcome.

1- Find a safe space to talk, outside of your familiar environment. Before you state anything, make sure that it comes from a place of empathy and love.

2- Share how you can take ownership of the situation. In my case, I shared that I had a lot of fun living with my friend, and a large part of me didn't want to let that go, yet I knew in my heart that I needed change if I was going to get to the next chapter in my life.

3- Acknowledge the person and your fears. I let my friend know how much I cared about her, how much she meant to me, and that I was scared about the transition.

4- Lastly, what can be the toughest part: a request for change, and a game plan. For my roommate, I let her know that we needed to live in separate places. I told her that I would immediately be looking to change the situation and wanted to ensure that the transition was as harmonious as possible. By creating an action plan, after the requested change, you are showing momentum into your vision and at the same time, asking the other person to honor that.

Your situation could relate to a co-worker and how they speak to you. It could be a relationship that needs to be changed or ended. It could be a family member whom you've allowed to talk to you in a certain way (and you take responsibility for it). Still, you are now taking ownership of the interactions and no longer allow negativity because you want your relationship based on support and love.

This simple yet sometimes emotionally difficult four-step process is a magic worker and does a phenomenal job at neutralizing heaviness between two individuals. Before practicing it, make sure to take a moment to thoroughly examine the root of the problem. Discover where you have ownership in it, as well as what harmonious outcome you want, before the discussion — this way, you have already envisioned some peaceful resolution beforehand, by setting your intentions.

Now that you have learned this tool for resolving conflicts and relationships, you know how to neutralize the emotional swings and the heaviness that can accompany them. Balancing the weight of these energetic conversations through the conflict and resolve process opens up your energy to the flow of a harmonious life full of presence, which ultimately brings you towards alignment.

It is vital to address the heaviness that's there, the "elephant in the room". There is no reason to waste energy on emotional stresses when it comes to conflicts. Have a beautiful conversation, and get that weight off your back! All we have is the present moment, at all times, and the stronger our presence, the more connected to the abundance of the Universe we will be.

Day Four: Clearing with Your Connections

First we'll go through your contact lists and start deleting the ones no longer serving you, conversely those you are no longer helping. Erase the ones of people you will most likely not be talking to again or at least shouldn't be talking to anymore. During this cleaning, you may have come across certain people and had an instant draw to call them and reconnect. You may also have experienced mixed emotions or anxiety around some of the names: possibly guilt for not reaching out, frustration because they haven't called you, discomfort about unresolved issues, or happy memories of the last time you had spent time together. These emotions are there for a reason; they can be like guideposts on a hike. Being aware of them allows you to be directed into action, if you so choose. You can achieve the same experience while going through past emails.

I remember how painful clearing out phone numbers a couple of years ago was for me. Many memories and emotions surfaced. The simple fact that, most likely, I wouldn't talk to the person again was saddening, even though I could have easily called them at random if I wanted to. I felt down all day, it was cathartic. Surprisingly, the following day I felt a sense of freedom that I didn't realize would be available.

Going through your contacts could take days, even weeks. Take time to start writing out a list of people you plan to reach out to and the immediate feelings that pop into your mind, as previously described. If you are an analytical person, you could even do this in a spreadsheet and sort your contacts based on emotions. Aim to truly understand your feelings and causes, do not brush over them.

Next, take responsibility for resolving any negative emotions between you and this person. Use the tools you've learned and go for it! Come from the heart, and don't forget to make a clear intention first. Who knows where the connection could lead, possibilities are endless.

However simple the project might seem, it could be stressful to know where to start. Imagine you had one week left to live: which five people would you be calling? Write them down. Get to it! When coming from your heart, from a place of love and wanting the highest and best for yourself and the other person, trust yourself that whatever you voice out-loud will work out beautifully. Trust is a massive part of the process when coming from an aligned place. Make it a goal to reach out to three people a day, at least. Don't get stuck in analysis paralysis; get on your accountability buddy for this book so you can remind each other of your commitments.

Remote Clearing

Clearing through your connections, you may also come across people that you feel it is best not to contact. If it is someone you don't feel safe reaching out to, or think that it will do more harm than good if you did reach out, you can work with something called the Ho'oponopono Prayer. People use this ancient Hawaiian prayer to take responsibility, ask for forgiveness, and send love. People use this prayer even towards a room and all the chairs in a space, for example, before speaking publicly in that room. Ask forgiveness. Send love to strangers from the past, present, and future.

How I use the Prayer:

First, I envision the person or his/her soul in front of me. You can also do this for yourself, as we tend to be so hard on ourselves! In this case, I would be asking myself and my soul for forgiveness, and I would look into my eyes in the mirror.

Then I state the following prayer in cycles of four (state the following four times) until I no longer feel the pressure of an energetic tie or pull.

"I'm sorry, please forgive me. Thank you for being in my life so that I may love you."

I know people who say the prayer more than forty times in a row, to fully resolve the tension between them and someone else. Pay attention to your body, it will tell you when the process is complete. You may experience lightness or release. You could also use this prayer before making that call or meeting with the person you want to clear with. When we take responsibility for healing and forgiveness with another, we open ourselves up to the newness that is aligned.

Some people say this prayer daily, as they get ready in the morning, in front of the mirror. I have said this prayer while driving to a meeting. Even though I didn't know who I was meeting and didn't have anything to apologize for, I prayed to add the warmth of a blessing. I had no idea of what was going on in their life at that moment, which could potentially cloud our moment together. The intention of the prayer supported clearing so that we could be present with each other.

Also, when I randomly think of someone, and the thought has frustration or some other disagreeable energy, I'll immediately push that negativity away by saying a prayer or sending them a bubble of love, envisioning it with intention.

When people wonder why I am positive all the time, this is a glimpse into my life. I don't like negativity. I prefer having no room for those lower vibrations in my life. Friends will say that I'm always "canceling" negative statements. I'm always sending love to people, even strangers I walk by, especially if I sense low vibe energy around them. They might look down or seem stressed out; one can never know what someone else's challenge might be. I have no idea if I changed their life at that moment, but I do hope that it became a bit lighter. You can also do this by saying something sweet and acknowledging or complimenting someone else. It is an instant shift to positive energy!

Today, begin with yourself. Choose to forgive yourself for any negative thoughts or pressures you have created. When you feel complete, move on to work with people around whom you felt stress.

The person whom you pray for with the Ho'oponopono Prayer may suddenly try to connect with you. However, since you are using this prayer to clear your relationship with individuals you didn't want to reach out, talk to, or meet with, you should honor your limits and do your best not to reach out. If needed, wait four days for the energy to subside. Do not be tempted.

When I decided to stop dating because I felt I met the one, exes and others whom I had dated randomly reached out. All at once! As if they knew that I was about to be taken away from them as a possibility. They felt the energy, even though they may not have known why. When you release people, they sense it. They probably have no idea what they are feeling, yet know something is up, so they think of you and reach out.

Here's another example: you think of someone, and then they call. Countless times, I have thought of someone and called them, only to hear them say that they had just been talking about me. Or, I get my phone to call someone, and it turns out they had just texted me.

Synchronicities are the energy of the Universe: we are all connected, and you will become more and more aware of this as you continue on your journey.

Day Five: Basic Body Energy Clearing

So far, we've been clearing external energies, and now we're embarking on a journey of internal energies. You will continue to become aware of your body by cleansing it of all negative energies. Before we go into clearing our body, it is critical to enter into a space of forgiveness and love towards our bodies.

Take ten minutes to tap into our body, practice love for each of its parts, and forgive yourself for all the difficulties you've put it through, all the discontent or anger you've experienced when you felt fat or unhappy with your body.

Think of how your body carries you: the body is unconditional, so strong, yet we often do not reward it with the love and care that it deserves. How often did you eat something you knew was wrong for you, or wouldn't bring ease and comfort to your body? How often have you pushed it farther than it wanted to go? I have lots of personal stories about taking advantage of my body instead of loving it.

In general, we are extremely harsh on ourselves. I have created a Ho'oponopono Prayer meditation, available on my website members page, that anyone can use to get in touch with their body. I recommend listening to the video of the Ho'oponopono Prayer for your body at least four times. You could also create one for yourself to listen to.

Practicing this allows you to forgive and love your body, thus encouraging it to enter into an optimum space of health and alignment, pruned and primed for giving constant advice, through its intelligence.

Throughout the day, start thanking your body, be in a state of gratitude. Yes, giving it gratitude for everything from digesting the food you are about to eat, for staying focused throughout the day as you work, for handling the long hours of sitting, etc. Honor your beautiful body with movement or exercise. According to my gifted physical therapist, our bodies love to move. He believes that going on a walk for fifteen minutes every morning resets our structural alignment. He refers to physical alignment and not the energetic one, yet it is all connected. He suggests that as we walk, we should have nothing in our hands: no coffee, no pulling dog, no cell phone or purse; the fifteen minutes are used for walking meditation, acknowledging our beautiful body, and setting the foundation for the day in gratitude! Our body deserves it. Movement shows how much we care and love it, so it can continue to serve us to its fullest potential.

You are on a journey of presence with our bodies. Our bodies deserve to be cherished. Awareness and presence serve our alignment in a significant way. It's a constant quest for me, and I am excited for you as this journey was one of my biggest lessons in life.

Day Six: Chakra Clearing

By now, you may wish to continue practicing the Ho'oponopono Prayer. It can quickly become part of your daily practice and morning rituals. We are going to build upon it further, in this chapter, with chakra cleansing.

First, let's add some sparkle to your life with colors! The first time I did this exercise, I felt it intensely, my fingers tingled, and my body felt the pressure as I moved my hands. I felt it most in my solar plexus, where people say that I radiate the most (a warm yellow color that happens to be my favorite color, along with gold).

We will not be going into details about chakras and their purpose, as the information is easily accessible to anyone.

The chakra clearing takes about ten to twenty minutes, depending on your experience. Read through the exercise first. Watch the video so you can step into regular practice. My favorite place to do this exercise is at the beach, with feet in the ocean, or while standing near a tree. The connection to the Earth via the environment supports the intensity of results. A video of this exercise is available on my website under book resources.

Wash Your Hands
You don't need to do this in water, go through the motions, holding the intention of purifying your hands by rubbing them together, air washing off the soap, negativity, and everything that does not serve you.

Ground Yourself
Place your feet hip-distance apart in a standing position where you feel comfortable. Imagine your body as a tree with feet rooted in the Earth. Your roots are going all the way to the center of the Earth, the core. I like to imagine that my roots are gold-colored.

These roots will be your connection to the Earth serving you in releasing all of the negative energy. Roots from your feet and legs continue into the Earth and act as a vacuum drawing all negativities to the core, where they transmute for the highest and best use. The Earth wants to support your healing and alignment always, accept the help of the Motherly Energy!

Bring Your Hands in Front of You

Have your arms rounded in front of you like you are holding a beach ball and your hands about ten inches in front of your pelvic floor. Hold your hands here while you envision a bright red light circling your hips. Imagine the red light cleansing you, and all the impurities being sucked out through your feet into the core of the Earth. You may feel warmth in your hands and possible movement within your body too.

When you feel complete, bring your hands up a few inches to your sacral chakra, which is your lower abdomen, below your belly button. Here, hold your hands at the same distance, and imagine a bright orange light circling your body. Feel all impurities being drawn out through your feet to the roots into the core of the Earth. Do this until you feel you've finished; it could easily be two minutes or longer.

Then bring your arms up to your third chakra, your solar plexus. See a bright yellow light circling your body, and while it does, it also continues to clear out all the impurities that do not serve your highest purpose.

Feel the experience, imagine the experience. I typically feel pressure as I pulsate my hands slowly from a few inches away from my body and farther out. It's almost as if I were kneading clay at a spinning wheel.

When you are ready, bring your hands up towards your chest, this is your heart chakra. See a bright green light circling you as your hands pulsate and feel yourself opening up your heart as you let go of all that doesn't serve you into the earth below you. Let it be transported out so that you don't have to carry this around with you any longer. Sometimes you'll feel pressure while you do this; if so, hold until you feel it expand, loosen, and shift.

As you feel clear within your heart, lift your hands to your throat chakra and see a bold, bright blue light circling your throat. This light is not only clearing your throat; it is opening up your voice so that you can speak the truth from your heart. You may feel your throat tighten, yawn, or cough immediately when doing this. Know that's a beautiful release that supports you.

Next, move your hands up to your face. Here's is my favorite part because it feels like a mind massage. Feel a violet-blue light circling throughout your mind. Continue to experience all the negative thoughts and impurities being sucked out through your feet, down the golden roots, into the center of the earth. They do not serve you and do not need to be a part of your life. When you feel complete, your mind comes to a state of relaxation and peace.

Finally, move your hands to your crown chakra, right above your head. Imagine a purple light, like an orb circling above you. You are allowing in the light of the heavens and Universe, the pure light of truth, into your body.

Recognize your crown as cleansed so that you can receive all that is in your highest being.

When you recognize your body as cleansed, start to feel a smile on your face, allow your arms to reach straight up into the "Winning Stance" or "Y" position. Let all the white purified light from the Heavens come into your body and then drop your hands towards the Earth. I do this three times for a complete clearing, allowing the light to eradicate any last bits that I may have missed. Let it all drop into the vacuum funnel of your golden roots, down into the core of the earth.

Lastly, raise your arms straight up again and slow spin as you drop your straight arms, creating a circular shield around you. I envision the shield being gold so that it reflects negativity that comes my way back out like a mirror, keeping me safe.

This chakra clearing meditation can be done daily, weekly, or monthly.

Don't let yourself be frustrated if you don't feel it the first time. There may be a lot of stuff to clear out before you start to feel it, or, like me, you may feel it strongly the first time and then less dramatically after.

Day Seven: News Diet

The news diet might be challenging for some. It's another practice of presence: avoid the news today, as well as any negative content (shows revolving around crime, hate, manipulation, lies). Negativity sells. As you become more present and aware of your surroundings, you may start to notice how much effect news can have on you.

For example, as I was reading this morning's news – my only 'news dose' every morning, an email that shows the headlines with half a sentence describing the topic - I immediately noticed the tingly sensation of fear entering my body. Of course, I instantly released the negativity that was creeping into my being because I know how much it doesn't serve me. You can get to this point of presence too.

The world feeds on this negativity, it draws emotions out of us, and people are instantly engaged. On an energetic level, watching negative things pulls down your vibration. As your vibration drops, you are projecting it out, whether you are aware of it or not, so it will also bring the vibes of those around you down. The opposite is true as well: when your vibrations raise, it affects many around you too.

When you are vibrating positively, you are also positively impacting people around you. When you are at a lower frequency, the same applies. For example, your being in a state of love and joy makes a powerful, positive impact on those around you.

One week, while I was sick, I chose to entertain myself by binge-watching a whole season of *Orange Is the New Black*. I allowed myself to get sucked in, being engulfed in the show, as I spent the week in bed. Once I was out and about feeling better, I noticed myself feeling the fears of being beaten up. I was continually looking over my shoulder, thinking someone was there to get me. I was sensing all these negative things from people who walked by, thinking about how they might attack me. In my mind, everyone was looking at me and not in a good way. It felt awful. Before that week, I'd happily walk down the sidewalk, probably smiling at everyone I passed by.

Similarly, a client of mine shared her experience of driving a lot in traffic while listening to podcasts. One particular week, she noticed something was off, she couldn't put her finger on it. Finally, something clicked in her that maybe that feeling was caused by the murder mystery podcast she got sucked into! She changed to a more uplifting, empowering station and experienced an immediate shift in her body and mood.

Unfortunately, people don't consciously sense how much they are affected. In my case, I now do clearings if I watch something negative, or I will fast forward through the negative parts. I can't have this energy following me as I'm super sensitive.

There is so much hatred, anger, violence, and fear beaming across our screens, and it only appears to be getting worse; hence, why it's so important to be present to your body. The more you meditate and notice how you feel around others, you'll sense how energy is affecting you at all times.

Pay attention to your energy level and your feelings, when negative headlines come into vision. For today, possibly tomorrow and forever, see how you can avoid the news and other programs that are bringing fear and violence into the world. If too difficult for you to accomplish, work to at least filter to only positive news.

Similar to taking a thirty-day vacation from gluten, seeing your stomach flatten out, and feeling more energetic, take a vacation from the harmful content.

There isn't a reason to watch a TV show that threatens your energetic being! You've got this, let that negativity out of your life, you will probably prefer it once you get the hang of it.

SUMMARY - ROOTS

Day One: Commit to a Clear Mind

- Intentionally commit to the work and to living with a clear mind.
- Pay attention to how often you are truly present in what you are doing.

Day 2: Taking Responsibility

- Take time to look back at moments where you have played a victim.
- Understand how you can take responsibility for these situations and find the silver lining.

Day 3: Equanimity

- Use the 4 Step Process to tackle any charged relationships and situations, so that you can remove the energetic weight from your body.

Day 4: Clearing with Your Connections

- Delete unnecessary contacts from your phone.
- Be aware during your conversations with others and notice how they make you feel.

Day 5: Basic Body Energy Clearing

- Use the Ho'oponopono Prayer to acknowledge every bit of your body. Love your body.
- When situations leave you feeling heavy or frustrated, imagine, from a 10,000-foot view, how you could take responsibility and use the Ho'oponopono Prayer.

Day 6: Chakra Clearing

- Watch the video and practice the chakra clearing meditation, take it outside, and feel free to listen to the video to guide you while doing the chakra clearing outdoors.
- Get into the Winning Stance regularly.

Day 7: News Diet

- Stay away from the news, headlines, social media, negative TV shows, books, music, and notice how your energy levels shift.

Don't forget to give thanks for everything continually!

*How did clearing your
roots raise your vibe?*

WEEK THREE – SUSTENANCE

Nurturing you

Trees consume water and minerals of the earth to stay alive, often for very long. An oak tree can age over 150 years, some surpassing 300 years. In less than a day during a flash flood, one could consume 120,000 gallons of water, preventing damage. So powerful!

One all-encompassing way to internally fuel your whole being - mind, body, and soul - is finding stillness, through meditation.

Opening to this presence, you will reap the rewards of feeling recharged as well as understanding, hearing, seeing, and exploring the guidance that's available to you via body intelligence. A daily advantage of fueling your body with the power of stillness is that when trauma hits, such as the flash flood to the tree, you can consume it and let it go with emotional resilience. The situations will start to roll off of you instead. Also, through meditation, you can have a calm, sustained energy that lasts. Some people can wake at 3 a.m., meditate for three hours or more and still feel like they had more than enough sleep.

The bottom line is meditate, don't medicate! There are numerous proven benefits of meditation that are beyond comprehension. Finding stillness is key to bringing in the body intelligence as it creates a foundation for the presence and listening. This week, you will learn several meditations which we will eventually use towards your guidance through body intelligence. Through these meditations, you can start exploring your environment and context, and play around with results gained throughout the week.

Day One: Notice Your Voice

Before we get to meditation, we will start paying attention to our inner voice. I'm not referring to your intuition, but rather to the voice in your head describing the world you are experiencing, as if you needed someone to narrate what you saw. It might be the voice that tells that you an outfit doesn't look right, and that you should change. The voice that says you ate too much after you finished a box of cookies. The voice that says a stranger's style is awkward, as you see them walk by you. The voice that states the obvious, but also the voice that shares random things that may or may not be true. It's noise, and it doesn't serve you.

Astonishingly, 80% of mental chatter throughout the day (approximately 60,000 thoughts)[3] is negative. Think about the extraordinary possibilities of reducing this even by 10%! It may be one of those days where you keep forgetting you were working on paying attention to your voice, and then it reminds you that you need to quiet it. Yet this underlying intention to pay attention has started the process as a new neural synapse in your brain, and you are on your way. Stopping the voice can be a difficult task as this inner dialogue has been a constant, until now! Noticing it is the first step. Next, command the voice to take a hike. The more consistently you quiet the voice, the smaller it will become, allowing presence to enter.

For example, my inner voice told me to keep writing as I was about to shut my laptop, and I listened to it. It only goes to show you that this is going to be a long journey, and we'll eventually learn to discern what works and what we can ignore. The voice has become less and less present for me. I do not know how long it takes to quiet the mind completely, but acknowledging it and being conscious of it is step one. Pay attention today. Pay attention to the thoughts that might be running through your mind, telling you should be doing this or that; then, choose to do what you prefer, such as reading a fantastic book on getting aligned. You are in control, so tell the noise "be gone!" Yes, it's that simple, say what works for you. My friends and family know I say "Cancel cancel" all the time:

---

[3] According to the Cleveland Clinic of Wellness - http://
www.clevelandclinicwellness.com/programs/NewSFN/pages/default.aspx?
Lesson=3&Topic=2&UserId=00000000-0000-0000-0000-000000000705

canceling statements which don't serve my highest and best purpose in well being as well as unnecessary interruptive thoughts.

It is vital to clear these thoughts because, as seen learned earlier, we should aim to be neutral at all times. In a state of neutrality, we can make decisions from a place of clarity. When we're listening to this inner voice that's continuously rambling, our choices do not stem from our awareness. The voice is typically composed of stories that we've made up, based on past experiences, or friends, family, and media. The voice will hold you back from the reality of NOW. As you recognize the differences, you can clear out the veil that clouds your reality of NOW and become in tune with your truth, stemming from alignment.

Day Two: Notice Your Body's Response

As you go about your day today, notice what you feel throughout your body. Hopefully, you've been doing the Ho'Oponopono Prayer Body meditation and also paid attention when feeling any negative weight. The meditations continue to support you towards getting in touch with your body. If you are still feeling disconnected, I encourage you to try Yoga Nidra.

Yoga Nidra is a practice where you concentrate on each part of your body, moving from your toes to your ankles, calves, knees, and so forth, all the way to your head, slowly, in a meditative state. My little addition of magic and healing to Yoga

Nidra is to imagine each part of your body illuminating with the power of pure healing white light as you work your way through your entire being. Many people also use Yoga Nidra as a method to peacefully fall asleep, but that is not our goal here. Vipassana meditation also focuses on observing the sensations in the body, in complete stillness and silence.

In my case, I initially had a lot of difficulties noticing my body's responses to life situations. Something awful would happen, and my coach would ask me "Where do you feel this in your body? What sensations are you experiencing?"

Whenever he asked me this, I would physically freeze up every time. I would instantly go numb as if I were in shock. There was a big disconnect between my psyche and body. I would wait for him to tell me where I was feeling it, and eventually, he'd say he was noticing tightness in the chest, or weight on the shoulders or neck. His response helped me break the frozen shock that I was experiencing so I could start to feel the specific sensations. My coach first recommended I practice Yoga Nidra to connect to each part of my body and my being.

One weekend, I ended up going to a three day, mostly silent workshop, where I learned to connect to my body. Funny enough, I wasn't even aware we were doing it at the time. People had been telling me I should become a coach and facilitate workshops, yet I had absolutely no interest in it. When I attended the workshop, however, it proved to be so life-shifting for me, I started to have a change of heart!

At the end of this workshop, I was so "high on life" that I felt I needed to share this with the world and at once, so that people could experience their truth as well because it was so freeing! Through the process of being present for three days, I had gained high awareness, yet I didn't even realize or understand it until the day after.

The Monday after, I sat down at my computer, working on a startup I had been running for almost seven years. I had already gone through multiple developers, gotten to sue someone to get money back that they had taken without performance, amongst other hurdles. There had been multiple empty promises made. Every startup has its ups and downs, and the number of challenges I had was proof of how out of alignment I was by not listening to body intelligence.

That morning, as I touched my computer keyboard, I felt immense heat running through my body. It was like an immediate 104-degree fever. I felt like my hands were in molasses as they tried to press the keys; it was challenging and very intense. My mind was in disarray about what was happening. I decided to take a break and go for a walk on the beach with my dog. When I got back, the same thing happened again. Being confused about it all, I decided not to work the rest of that day and give myself a break for reintegration to reality after a powerful workshop. The following day, however, I had the same experience.

Five years prior, when I was 30, I had been told by my gynecologist that I wouldn't be able to have kids because my hormones had flat-lined to levels below normal ranges. The news was devastating. I have since tackled this with naturopathy, acupuncture, tinctures, and now my hormones are at happy levels. I am sharing these details because, when I again felt this immense heat and molasses running through my body, on the second day of trying to work on my startup, I had an epiphany. Quite possibly, this had been happening the whole time that I had been working on the startup, and I wasn't aware of it until I found some truth by listening to my body, during the silent workshop.

It was no wonder that this kind of awful heat running through my body would create dis-ease and flat line my hormones. There was no room for health and harmony in my body while this immense fire was running through it. Sometimes the heat is positive, yet as you become present, you will be able to discern good and bad feelings in your body.

Today is all about getting in touch with your body, connecting to it, from this point on, and forever! Your body is a guiding force throughout all of life. And it doesn't need to take you more than two years to realize it, like in my case.

Start to notice how your body feels when you wake up, how your body responds when you start checking your emails, get some news, or a heartwarming phone call. Be in touch with heat, posture, tenseness, heart rate changes, emotional changes, weight, pressure, food cravings, etc. Did you know that most food cravings are caused by unmet emotional needs, fears, and excitement? Your body intelligence is communicating and guiding you through it all.

If you aren't feeling sensations within, take a moment to consciously check in with your body, from your toes to ears. Do a body scan, filling up each part of your body with white loving light. You can easily do this in 90 seconds or less. There are a multitude of benefits for pausing throughout your day to accomplish this. I have a meditation available for you on my website under the book resources as well to take three minutes to connect.

Today is about being aware and present, and I strongly encourage you to make this your practice for life. After all, it only takes twenty-one days to form a habit. You can do it!

Day Three: Meditations

We want to keep this awareness of our bodies going. Don't hesitate to stop any of the lessons. Taking a break is A-Okay. All the exercises will bring your practice deeper so that you can lead with your intuition, regardless of what challenges or obstacles come your way, each day.

There are many forms of meditation, and I'm always getting asked "Where do I start?" In this section, I'll share with you some of my favorite types of meditation. There is no right or wrong way to do this. I am continually switching it up. The bottom line is *just do it*!

Guided Meditation

When you have trouble getting your mind to relax, sometimes it's best to listen to an audio meditation, similar to the Ho'oponopono body prayer. Your brain might still wonder, which the meditation might even instigate, but for many, this will support quieting the external noise.

I create meditations for myself and work with the disKNEKT service as they bring a customized coaching element into the meditation; there are many others, for health, weight loss, abundance, and so much more. One of the reasons I use them is for grounding and connection to the earth and the Universe.

A friend, Soho House, and Private Celebrity Chef Shane Fatemian started listening to a guided meditation involving breath work on the meditation app. Every morning for over a year, he completed this meditation. Then he decided to run a marathon, and during the run, he found himself doing the same breathing process. Compared to previous races he had done, he completed this one in record time with the least amount of training. Because he had listened to the meditation every morning for over 365 days in a row, it had become second nature to his body, which allowed him to go faster than before. His body was aligned when bringing the breathwork into practice, and he knew how to conquer the great feat of running 26.2 miles with ease.

This story exemplifies the power of creating a ritual in stillness every day. All forms of presence for ourselves and our bodies support powerful rejuvenation and connection to the oneness that we are.

Silent Meditation

Whether you enter into a quiet meditation for two minutes or two hours (I do have friends that do this each morning around 3 a.m.), you'll soon start reaping many benefits.

Find a comfortable place to sit, with your back erect as it supports your nervous system, which promotes healing in your body. It can be awkward at first as many rarely sit or stand straight in the first place. Don't worry; your muscles will strengthen over time.

In one particular silent meditation retreat that I did, we went up to an hour of silence, multiple times throughout the day. My whole body was sore the next day. By the third day, though, I had become comfortable in my position. I sat with my legs crossed on the floor, propped up on a pillow. The elevation supported me in having a straight back.

Another choice is a kneeling bench where you can sit comfortably with the knees on the floor and the legs folded underneath. It is my favorite position. Look up "kneeling meditation bench" online, should you choose to purchase one for your practice.

Choose what position works best for you, and remember that it will get easier the more you do it. I recommend starting by setting your timer for ten minutes. Tell yourself you aren't going to do anything else for those ten minutes so that you can set your mind up to win.

If this is your first or even your 100th time, you might find your mind wandering and thinking about all the things you aren't getting to, or about some creative ideas you feel the need to write down immediately. Stay in the space of knowing you'll remember the thought after the ten minutes. When thoughts arise, simply focus on your breath along with the expansion and contraction of your belly. Be in the space of clearing your mind, but if it's just too hard, in the beginning, keep going back to your breath and belly. Feel your breath bringing in oxygen that nourishes your body. You may even feel a tingly sensation.

When breathing isn't working, try bringing your middle and thumb fingers together on each hand — as your mind starts to drift, slowly come back to the sensation and connection between these two fingers, which may feel slightly tingly or warm. It's about getting into a neutral, thoughtless position.

Aim at doing ten minutes a day, then, after a week, move up to twenty minutes each day. A recommended practice is twenty minutes in the morning and twenty at night. The ritual allows you to fully connect and ground yourself in this world. Also, as you go through the day, you can easily choose to pause for two minutes of silence. I like to think of it as rebooting a computer so that it runs efficiently and smoothly again. Just set your timer for two minutes, knowing that everything else can wait.

Try waking up earlier to allow your mind this calmness before the day. According to some studies, meditation can be more rejuvenating for your psyche and body than sleep[4].

Mantra Meditation

Mantra meditations consist of affirmations, such as "I am free", "I am love", "I let go" are often translated from Sanskrit, and used in yoga practice. For example, Kundalini yoga incorporates mantras and breathwork to activate the Kundalini channel within, a divine spiritual life force. I enjoy a Kundalini class once in a while for experiencing the unique sensations inside. After a Kundalini class, one can't help but feel aligned with life. Such a class can also work as a complement to the methods presented throughout this book.

My first experience with mantra meditation was my discovery of the *21 Day Meditation Experience*, a collaboration between Deepak Chopra and Oprah Winfrey. I walked with my dog along the boardwalk and found a bench to plop myself down on, feet in the sand, overlooking the ocean. The first part of the meditation is guided, and then we are lead to silence and practicing a specific mantra. I quietly said the mantra given, out loud, and within a few minutes, I felt like I was teleporting. My

---

4 Melatonin increases 98% via meditation, and in one study up to 300%.
https://eocinstitute.org/meditation/require-less-sleep-with-meditation-460

mind and body went fuzzy, and I experienced being 100% energy, not solid. Within seconds, I snapped out of the experience because this was new territory for me, I was nervous, and it was my first time feeling that way. It doesn't happen every time for me. However, it is beautiful, and nowadays, when it does, I embrace it fully.

A powerful mantra that you can try out is "So Hum" meaning "I am that" where "that" is the Universe; the mantra helps connect to the oneness that is. Repeat "So Hum" again and again. This meditation couples the mantra with breathing – breathing in for SO and breathing out for HUM. Your mind might try to take you elsewhere, come back to the mantra. Explore this type of meditation to figure out which mantra matches your style – and then commit to it. You can also find other mantras that resonate with you.

Sanskrit mantra meditations support opening up the Prana, Chi, or Life Force within. Just like mantras, this book intends to help bring about an awareness of our body, presence, and honor our internal compass.

Day Four: Movement Meditation

Many don't consider exercise meditation. I do, and it's my favorite kind! Our bodies are meant to move. You weren't designed to sit in front of a computer all day and in front of a TV all night. The body is built for movement: running, walking, hiking. Besides, connecting with nature is one of the best things for us because a green environment lives in harmony, and it promotes being in balance. Getting into nature provides an opportunity for us to absorb the harmony as well. For example, this morning, I was feeling a little stagnant and knew I just had to get outside. Once I did and was amongst the eucalyptus trees, breathing in their aroma, I had a smile of gratitude on my face. So easy!

Movements such as dancing, with or without music, can get your body into a mesmerizing space where you just let go and allow your body the freedom to do what it wants. Sometimes I turn off the lights and light a few candles with the intention to have the highest and best vibrations within my space. Then I turn up the music and dance my heart out. It might be for one song, or possibly ten, my body instantly feels fully connected and aligned with my mind and soul.

Once I got a thirty-day pass to a hot yoga studio and committed to going every morning with a friend, while it was still dark outside. It was amazing to notice the studio getting lighter and lighter as the sun came up. Each morning, the teacher would direct us through the same Bikram poses, and about three weeks in, she asked if we minded doing the sequence in silence. She said that doing it in silence might unleash some emotions, and she wanted to make sure we were all on board.

I usually get asked by my friends why I don't get more emotional about this situation or another. So, knowing how un-emotional I was, I figured I wouldn't be affected by the change in the routine. Well, a little over an hour into the silent yoga experience, I started crying and didn't stop until the next week.

This was happening around ten months after my ex and I had chosen to get divorced. My friends and family had been wondering why I wasn't emotional throughout this troubling process, why I wasn't crying on the bathroom floor, or crying myself to sleep at night. Well, I shared I didn't feel it my style. Once we had decided to move forward with the divorce, instead of being with myself, as some may have, I dove into a startup project, while also working as a real estate agent. These distractions didn't allow me any time to fully feel and understand what was going on below the surface. Apparently, I had a lot of pain from the divorce, and the emotional outpour after the silent Bikram yoga was proof of it.

Since this experience, I have understood how important it was for me to use silence or instrumental music to guide me, whenever I feel that emotions are somewhere deep down. It supports me in getting them to rise to the surface so I can release them. Since then, I have emotionally evolved, and now most of the time, whenever feelings are present, I can experience them and release them with much less effort.

Emotions are meant to be felt and expressed. The dis-ease of emotions can actually lead to disease. My stage four cancer clients have shared their observations and correlations from past situations with me. As you go through the journey of experiencing your being, your body, your light, you'll be incredibly in tune with what it is your body desires, guiding you in truth and alignment.

For many, gardening, painting, and cooking can also be a meditative experience. By getting into a singular focus while moving, you disconnect. Similar to hiking in the harmony of nature, connecting with the earth through gardening also grounds you in balance. Connecting with the food you eat is another essential part of oneness. Talking and "combing" the fruits and veggies with your fingers programs them to deliver the specific nutrients that your specific body needs to fight disease. Besides, it's another reason to do your cooking and pour love into everything you do.

One day I was rear-ended in a car accident while waiting for a light to turn green. It was a light tap, yet it's incredible how much that little tap affected me. I had constant headaches, so my doctor let me know I had experienced a concussion, or swelling of the brain. She wanted me to stop working, stop looking at my phone, stop reading or doing anything with my eyes for a month so that I could let my brain relax. Talk about detox! I had about fifteen real estate clients. You can imagine that wasn't an option for me. So I did the best I could to limit myself, because this headache was constant.

Weeks after the accident, my friend Ruben invited me to come and paint a mural with him at the Beverly Connection in Los Angeles. As an artist, it can be challenging to work within the lines, especially on someone else's art piece. I was to paint a sketched image with the words "Create Your Moments" on the wall, tracing his outline. I zoned in and focused on staying within the lines, just so. I didn't want to create any catastrophes, only beautiful moments.

After three hours or so of painting in a meditative, focused space, I was cleaning up and noticed that my headache had completely disappeared! Even better, it didn't come back. There were other issues from the accident that persisted; however, the headaches vanished. I could function without that overbearing annoyance.

Meditation heals. Get present with the body and mind while in movement. Remove distractions from your environment - your phone, watch, etc. Move yourself in silence, feel your beautiful body move, and experience it. Let chance thoughts float away, enjoy!

Day Five: Rebooting

If you're anything like me, you wake up with a million things to do. Even though 95% of the time I have time for myself during my power hour in the morning, there are days I wake up to "emergencies" that need addressing right away. Today was one of those days. I woke up to a text from a client who was canceling our appointment. The meeting involved other people, so I needed to phone them and re-schedule.

My morning routine was immediately out of the window. I noticed that as the day got going, I wasn't feeling grounded. The serenity I usually felt was lacking, since I hadn't taken time to myself, to begin with. We've all been there: constant distractions from all angles can quickly take us away from our planned schedules.

Even if your day does start on the right foot, possibly by early afternoon, you might be feeling differently. Especially if the day isn't going the way you'd like it to. Here's an excellent time for a reboot meditation.

Think of our computers or cell phones. When they get slow or freeze, the first thing we do or are told to do is to power them off, restart and see if anything changes. Reboot! Our brilliant minds love a little rebooting also.

I first learned this from a friend who runs a few companies. We met for dinner one evening, and he told me he had gone to the beach early for a fifteen minutes reboot because he didn't want to bring any of his chaotic work energy into our time together. He told me he does this before every meeting, even if it's in the car, for only two minutes. This practice has stuck with me ever since.

It's astounding how powerful taking a moment before meeting with others or going into a workout can be. Take a moment to breathe consciously, to be in silence, to feel gratitude, to set an intention for what you're looking to bring into the next period of your life, regardless of what it is. It's like an intentional resetting prayer.

I put my hands in prayer form in front of my heart, take three to ten breaths, putting pressure on each finger after my deep belly breath, while holding the intention of what's to come.

It is my reboot. My goal is to do it all day long; however, I probably do it once or twice a day.

This rebooting practice is super powerful when you're feeling an overwhelming emotion. Let's say you're feeling upset because you just got some awful news, yet you're about to go and meet some friends and don't want to bring that depressing energy with you. Taking a moment to acknowledge the pain or frustration allows it to move through you and out at a faster pace than if you ignored it and pressed it down, which not only harbors the emotion, but also expands it. When I got divorced, I had subconsciously pushed my emotions deep down and ignored feelings in my body, until they burst during a silent Bikram yoga session.

Pausing also supports your grounding throughout the day, allowing you to reconnect with your self. By doing this, you become more present and aware of how your body is reacting to things during the day, thus opening up your experience of body intelligence and alignment via guidance, the goal of the book.

Days Six and Seven: Practice Meditations

Meditation is powerful and supports your alignment and attention to body intelligence, so play around enjoying all of these meditations.

SUMMARY - SUSTENANCE

Day 1: Notice Your Voice
• Stay in tune with your inner dialogue, notice the thoughts that pop up and prevent you from experiencing the reality of what is.

Day 2: Notice Your Body's Response
• What's happening with your body right now?
• Notice the feelings, sensations, and temperature of your body as you go about your day experiencing challenges, emotions, and thoughts.

Day 3: Meditations
• Play around with different meditations to see what style resonates with you most.
• Pick one type of meditation and stick to it. Gradually go from ten to twenty minutes in your sessions.

Day 4: Movement Meditation
• Try dancing in silence, going to a silent yoga class, cooking in silence with love, hiking in silence without your phone or other distractions.
• Move and be with your self.

Day 5: Rebooting

- Take time to breathe in and out, consciously, throughout the day, whenever you transition, from work to play to cooking to children to adulting, whatever the transition. Count each finger, taking ten deep breaths while putting pressure on each finger, creating an intention for the next moment of the day.

Days 6 & 7: Practice Meditations
- The goal is to make this a daily practice. It may feel overwhelming at first, but it will become second nature in the end.

Notice your energy levels after fueling your body with stillness.

WEEK FOUR - TRUNK
YOUR CORE

The trunk of a tree connects the roots to the crown of the tree. Similarly, your core connects you to the world beyond you and communicates with it.

During this communication process, you must be extremely clear about your goals, so that your truth is unwavering, and clear action can follow. Getting clear on what the truth is entails the use of body intelligence. This week, you will figure out if your body agrees with your dreams, if are they in alignment with your path. You've got to know your truth.

Speaking in fairytale storybook terms, doesn't every girl want the fancy wedding and the perfect family with pictures to prove it, while the guy, breathtakingly handsome, of course, is trying for multi-millionaire status so he can demonstrate his worth? So cliché. Problems arise from these generalities and the lack of specifics when it comes to dreams and desires. Zooming in on one's goals, down to the nitty-gritty details, is what this chapter is all about. Once you are clear, you can start to fine-tune the experience and check in with your body to see if it is aligned. Often times the body is shouting directions, and people aren't listening, like when I was working on my startup, and my body was screaming NO for years until I finally became aware of its voice.

Your goals could be an outlandish challenge to achieve, or you might only need to fine-tune small details to get the desired results. When people are in alignment with their aspirations via their body intelligence, situations start to synchronistically line up and manifest like magic. They are what Carl Jung, founder of analytical psychology, defined as 'meaningful coincidences'.

Day One: Best Day Ever

Today's going to be so good! Before I start coaching clients on an individual level, I ask them to complete this exercise. It gives us a basis for the next steps, and I'll guide you through it this week, so you can be empowered through self-guidance.

Yes, you are one step closer to alignment with your goals! Getting into alignment with your desires starts with the pure intention to create results and open up space for all those dreams to enter and unfold. And that is what the tools in this book are designed for. You are open to receive; even if you don't believe it, play along and pretend you do.

Have fun here, as this is meant to be a joyous process. For this exercise, you're going to need your journal. You are going to start doing a lot of writing from here on out, so find a journal you love and are excited to open up.

Set aside 30-45 minutes to do this exercise, get comfortable so that imagination flows effortlessly out of you. First, connect yourself and your being, your soul. Sometimes I touch my heart and then my head to connect my heart and mind through physical intention. I do this every time I start writing my book, to fully ground myself in being a conduit for the message to come forth to paper.

Write down the specific details of a day in the life you want to create. Be very detailed, as we are going to use this for many other things throughout this process. This activity is a foundational one. For example: you are waking up in 1000 thread count sheets to a magical kiss on your shoulder, before you get out of bed. You must get extremely specific: what smells are you sensing? How's the weather? You must be able to feel this experience, the joy, the smiles on your face, etc.

This day is not a vision of you on vacation, unless your dream life is one where you are always traveling. Rather, this should be an example of what next Tuesday would look like if you were living a life you would feel completely fulfilled and satisfied by.

Enjoy this experience, let your body light up, and your face show how much you love this day, with a beautiful smile of gratitude. Become immersed in this dream day and let it all out on paper!

Day Two: Itemizing Your B.D.E.

Hopefully, you found yesterday's experience to be fulfilling and rewarding as you become more and more present to what your body is communicating with you. Today we are going to take it one level deeper. For each line of text, go through what is needed to accomplish and achieve that item. Note the characteristics of the experience.

Create two columns: "Accomplishments" and "I am" and then go through and break down your beautiful day. For example, in my dream vision, I see myself writing and meditating each morning with my fatty bulletproof coffee, nestled up in a cozy blanket on the balcony as I admire the beach view and listen to the hypnotic trance of the waves crashing.

ACCOMPLISHMENTS	I AM
I have acquired a beach home with a balcony and a beautiful view.	I AM prosperous, satisfied and successful.
I meditate daily.	I AM present with abundant time.

It will take a bit of time to break it down line by line. Trust it is all part of the alignment process, so get excited for those new a-ha! moments you're about to have.

Tomorrow we have another level to build upon with your Best day ever. You must acknowledge the traits that you have in this present moment. If you don't feel that "you are" them yet, start saying them as part of your journey of affirmations. Each of the I AM statements is creating new neural synapses in your brain, which will support you in the long term. I spend about five minutes a day on affirmations, and then they start to come up throughout the day. I'll be in a conversation with someone, and then they will refer to the adjective I am using to describe myself in my affirmations. It happens all the time. It's pretty magical, and to me, it confirms that this works.

To solidify the I AM traits, you can also go down memory lane to times when you had accomplishments that gave you this feeling, so that you know you are worthy of saying and acknowledging it. This is just as important, as there are always past wins in your life you can pull from, but sadly many people put the weight on the negative things. Remember the good times as well! Sometimes you just need to write down all your accomplishments to remind yourself how amazing you are.

These exercises can be difficult as they may create resistance. However, the new neural pathways being created in your brain will help you bring about your desired dream day with so much more ease. The I AM affirmations are an introduction to your mind's eye and the realization that you may not have spent time recognizing or acknowledging these qualities within yourself previously.

For bonus magic, work on applying feelings to the statements; this will support your process as well.

Day Three: Truth is Light, Lies are Heavy

Today, we start to take guidance from our bodies! Ancient Egyptians believed that our wisdom and soul were in the heart and that our brain was just gelatinous. Maybe they were onto something?

All right, now take a moment to meditate on the following two scenarios, one at a time. After you read one scenario, close your eyes and see it happening like a movie in your mind, notice the responses in your body. These are deciding indicators of the fine-tuning we're doing. Take the time to feel each reaction within and practice the meditations without distractions.

You'll want to find a quiet place to take this all in and experience it within.

Scenario 1:

It's early in the morning, and you've woken up about an hour earlier than usual because you start hearing this steady stream of water. You crankily get out of bed and walk towards the kitchen where you notice there has been a leak, and water is gushing everywhere. You don't know what to do. It's too early; you will have to call company emergency numbers for support. You are frustrated because you woke up early and had inspiring plans for the day that will most likely need canceling so you can deal with this mess.

How does this feel?

What sensations do you experience as you read the story?

I'm sure you have negative stories of your own you can pull from the past to explore the responses in your body.

Scenario 2:

You were out and about today running errands, which went surprisingly smooth, including rock star front row parking. Everyone has been extraordinarily kind and complimentary to you, even strangers. When you get home, there is a huge bouquet from a special someone, "just because" they wanted you to know how special you are. Then you go out for dinner with a friend and just for kicks and giggles try to get into this new restaurant that everyone has been raving about. You've heard it's tough to get into, but figure it's been a great day so far, so why not just ask? You make the call and find out there was a cancellation, and they can fit you right in! It's been such a phenomenal day, you feel like the luckiest person!

Do you have a smile on your face?

What are you feeling in your body?

Are you having issues feeling sensations in your body?

Notice the differences in responses in your body. Maybe do one of your meditations, Yoga Nidra or the Ho'oponopono Body prayer, to get in touch with your body again.

You can also try sitting in silence or even lying down, getting comfortable, and repeating Yes, Yes, Yes, Yes, Yes. Keep repeating it out loud until you feel it in your body. What do you notice? It could be tingling, expansiveness, pure lightness, a pull, or warmth. What is it for you? I feel sensations all along the right side of my body, more specifically in my gut. When I'm super present, I feel it from head to toe on my right side.

Then try the opposite, saying NO, NO, NO, NO, NO. Again, repeat it until you are clear on the sensations happening in your body: possibly a tightness somewhere, or a contracting, restrictive movement, pressure, or heaviness. What's the experience you are having?

Think of a baby or toddler who's upset. What do you see? An infant that's stretched out and stiff and feeling heavier in weight while they scream. A child who's standing tall yelling with hands clenched. It's the embodiment of a definite NO as your body tightens and constricts. Something is out of alignment. You may even notice yourself making a fist while in conversation, once in a while. When I was in a bad relationship, a therapist noticed I was making fists when talking to him. I didn't even notice! These are sensations to be noticed. Truth is light, and lies are heavy.

Some of my clients will close their eyes and see the color green or red for Yes or NO. Others will stand tall and will feel a Yes by leaning forward, and a NO by a pull backward. Find out how your body communicates to you.

For me, it was upsetting to realize that it took me two years to truly trust my body, while my clients can get it in one sitting, when we do energy work. If you're like me, don't worry, don't give up and learn to trust.

Trust is probably the biggest block for people, as it so clearly was for me. Trust is the first concept we learn as a baby. We're entirely dependent on others. If this trust was broken when you were young, even in your first hours, there might be some additional healing work to be done. I find it as something needing acknowledgment when doing energy healing for clients. I'll work back to the point where they were conceived or born unto this Earth.

Don't let your fears hold you back from listening to your body. This section could be the best part of this book, as once you've got this down, you can start using it for every decision you make. I use this from choosing what to order at restaurants to making big decisions for the day. Many times clients and friends ask me what my gut says for them. Although I answer, I also lead them to listen to their bodies so they can feel an individual response as well.

Should you want to triple check yourself, I'll teach you about muscle testing, also called applied kinesiology. Many naturopaths, chiropractors, acupuncturists, and energy healers use this as a way to have our body respond instead of us possibly projecting our thoughts. I usually listen to my gut for everything; however, sometimes I'll question things if there is a lot of heaviness around the decision, as I know I have the power to create whatever answer I want as well. In these situations, I'll triple check by muscle testing with my hands, further proof that our body has the answers.

There are multiple ways to muscle test. I'm going to teach you the one with your hands. I do want to reiterate how important it is also to continue listening to the rest of your body. Before moving forward, remember that when you ask questions, you are asking in the present moment and for yourself. To ask questions for others, you need their permission. To ask for future situations, know that answers you receive are here to support your present, which may guide you in a direction, yet not necessarily the finite destination.

Let's say you are wondering whether planning a trip to Italy is in the flow of Alignment. So you'd ask 'Is it in my highest and best interest to start planning this trip to Italy, now? Is it in my highest and best interest to book airline tickets today for this trip happening in two months?' These are examples of how to turn future questions into questions for the present.

For muscle testing with hands, bring your index and thumb together on your left hand, and your index and thumb together on your right hand. You are making the "everything is A-OK" symbol with both hands. Then link the two circled fingers together and ask a Yes or No type question[5].

Start with something simple such as 'My name is_____.' I would say 'My name is Bethany.' When stating this and trying to break the two loops, there is a lot of strength. When I say 'My name is Elliot' my fingers break apart with ease. Feel free to continue playing around with this and the forces between your fingers. Pause before asking another question, so there isn't any extra energy lingering from the previous one.

Remember that our minds are phenomenally powerful and that you can control the outcome of the answer too. When asking, be present, and notice if you are swaying the answer, be detached from what the response is when asking the question. If you state a question while thinking to yourself that you want a Yes, then most likely that is what you'll get. It's another reason why it's terrific to do this with friends so you can be unattached from results and answers. I will also pause and state to myself "I surrender to truth." The goal, of course, is to be so present and neutral.

From today onward, ask your body, and feel the answer. I have clients who tell me years later how life-changing this has been for them in all their decision making, goals, and plans. These body responses are what you want to guide your alignment.

_____

[5] See the video on my website for clarity.

Day Four: Tweaking the Good and the Bad

Now that you have your Best Day Ever charted out with traits and goals, along with a new understanding of truth and lies, Yes and NO, we will use this part of the alignment process to go through each item and decide whether:

A- You feel you have those traits now

B- The goal is alignment for you

When I ask "Are you aligned with your dreams?" I'm talking about whether the particular desired experience is something you can achieve with ease, versus challenges that feel like climbing a mountain. Not that you can't do the climb, but it is important that there be flow and harmony when considering the starting point, where you are currently in your life.

For example, a client had a house on her list of goals. She felt that the house was going to be somewhere in Manhattan Beach, CA, and she would live there with her man, yet I was getting a NO answer from my body. We couldn't figure out why. So we tweaked the house and changed its location to just the beach vs. a specific location. Within months, she had the opportunity to purchase a home that reflected her vision... in Costa Rica. Regardless, the house was on the beach!

Compare tweaking goal statements to tuning an old radio, adjusting the knob to get the station to come through. I call this fine-tuning or tweaking your goals, so that they are aligned.

Things can change all the time, so the priorities of your dream and decision making will adjust as well. Figure out what's in alignment with you at the present moment so you can continue forward instead of struggling to figure out why you aren't getting a Yes on something you want.

Break up your phenomenal day list! Go through each item and take a moment to feel what your body says. Are you getting warm fuzzy feelings, negative feelings, or nothing at all? Listen to your body. Go through the items, one at a time, to get a Yes or a NO. If you are getting good vibes, you know it's a Yes. Your body intelligence is sharing that you are already in alignment.

If you get nothing, then it's not necessarily good or bad, just not strong enough to bring about a response. Just leave it for now, you can come back to it as we continue to build on your Best Day Ever, in the next chapters.

If you get a NO or uncomfortable feelings, then try tweaking and fine-tuning your goal, as we did with my client and her house. See what you can do to change that negative experience to a cozy feeling. Note that you should do this in a place that isn't charged with too much emotion already. Your home should be a great place for it, if you've cleared it all out. However, if you feel it's necessary, you may want to find that cathedral environment, maybe a nature park, to take your time and run through this so you can pay attention to what your body is saying.

Recently, I had a client go through this exercise with me. She was getting a Yes for every sentence, while I wasn't, when checking my own body. as we went through her list together. The reason could be that the exercise deals with 'a day in your best life', so of course, it's going to feel warm, cozy, and exciting. It's imperative to be super clear and neutral so that you can make the necessary tweaks and adjustments. Tap into a different awareness of your day, one of discernment. If you are getting Yes's for everything, why haven't these things happened yet? Double-check, maybe even triple check, depending on your emotional state, over the next few days to make sure you're 100% clear. Sometimes I'll make a spreadsheet to look over a few days to make sure that I'm aligned.

This exercise may take some time, yet I know you've got this! I see many people get to the place of understanding what they have to do. It can be your new trick for everything: what does your body say? Good or bad? Trust it completely. Surrendering to your body's responses might feel testing at first, but the more you surrender, the more synchronistic your life will become. You'll experience life from a space of grace and ease.

Day Five: Read, See, Verbalize, and Experience

Now that you have fine-tuned your dream day, write it out again as a story, so that you can read it daily.

Since you know your body is aligned with this vision, feel yourself tingling with joy, love, gratitude and surrender as you read your vision each day. Another way to experience this beautiful dream day is to allow it into your life is by reading it out loud, playing it out in your mind so that you can experience it with eyes closed, feeling the movie of your life take place.

We want those neural pathways fully developed, so they steer your awareness in the aligned direction of your goals! Your vision is meant to manifest, it will carry you forth in revealing all that is in your highest and best interest.

One way I tap into my dream is by reading my vision out loud so I can visualize it and feel it at the same time. Sometimes, before I go to an event, I'll tap into the Best Day Ever so that I can fully align myself to what I am creating at that moment. By doing this, I'm giddy and full of joy before I walk in, and I also know I'm turning myself into an aligned manifesting magnet to meet those who are harmonious with my vision for this dream day.

Day Six: When You're Not Feeling It

There are times when I meditate on my vision and don't feel it at all. And days when I skip the meditation because I allow life to happen instead of consciously choosing to be in the desired space.

When this happens, I know that my vibration is off and that I'm not open to receive. It means I have contracted and restrictive energy and get to open it up like a blossoming rose. When I "allow life to happen", I'm coming from a go-with-the-flow place, yet it also could be a state of reactiveness. You don't want to always be in surrender, you want to be at the point of co-creation.

When we expand our energy, we reconnect with the force of the Universe from a conscious mindset, which creates a sensation of openness to the gifts that are here for us to receive. As you blossom and expand your energy field, you are re-aligning yourself. In recent weeks, my favorite practice is to get outside and connect with nature, even if it's just a walk breathing in the fresh air. Uniting with nature, knowing that we are all one and connected, will bring you back to balance.

Think of your hand in a fist which doesn't even allow water to run through it. Your energy field is similar when contracted, and it stops your intentions from flowing in. There is power in every single moment and thought you have. Typically, when going through a contracted experience, you tend to be in automatic mode, going from experience to experience without even really noticing. You may also be living from your subconscious or victim state. Open your arms wide, be grateful, and allow for all that you choose to come to you. At the same time, when you are open and expansive, negative things won't affect you nearly as much.

I was talking to a psychologist friend about how people can become so consumed by negative things that it carries into their next day and the next. We were talking about how sometimes many negative things tend to happen at the same time: deaths, job loss, breakups, etc. I had noticed this happening all around me and thought "Why is everyone around me living such traumatic situations, but not me?". I became aware that I actually did have traumatic situations happen the previous week, but they hadn't affected me the way they did others.

Becoming neutral about what some consider negative situations, shifts our reality. I am empowered to keep rolling on, like the waves in the ocean. Being on a higher vibration level supports this. Also, when people are in a happy space, they tend not to notice the negative stuff. What you focus on expands. Are you thinking from a positive space or a negative one?

Let's get you to at least neutral so that you are open to allowing these dreams and goals to flow into your life.

Day Seven: The Bigger Picture - Purpose

One of the workshops I have facilitated for companies revolves around connecting your personal vision to the company's vision. Many people work only for the stability that a steady paycheck brings them and their families. They continue working, whether they enjoy the position or not.

One aspect of Organizational Development within companies is creating productivity and efficiency through human capital. During my workshops, we address the mission and vision of the company. Then, we go over personal goals. When we break down our individual goals - similarly to the "I

AM" statement exercise - we notice that they typically have to do with experiencing love, connection, and supporting others. We then connect the two, our own goals and the company's vision, and find inspiration.

I believe that all our core purposes are to experience joy, freedom, and love. To figure out what your core purpose is, just keeping asking yourself WHY?

For example:

Dream: *I want this book to reach millions.*
Q: I then ask myself, WHY?
A: Because instead of being influenced by others, I want everyone to know their truth.
Q: WHY?
A: When people operate from their truth, they will experience freedom, and the vibration of the planet will rise to foster joy, thus less violence.
Q: WHY?
A: Because we'll have a planet of love, people will know their truth and will be in love with themselves, which will spread.
Q: Why do I want this book to reach millions?
A: I want more love in the world.

We ended at love- BOOM!

Now you try it and see where you end up!

SUMMARY - TRUNK

Day 1: Best Day Ever

• Get your journal out and fully immerse yourself in letting out the vision of your perfect day. Write out so many details that anyone could read it and have the same idea and possibly a similar visceral response as you.

Day 2: Itemizing Your Best Day Ever

• Line item out your Best Day Ever into accomplishments and I AM statements.

• Repeat the I AM affirmations for about five minutes every morning.

Day 3: Truth is Light, Lies are Heavy

• Engage with different scenarios and exercises to develop your body's Yes and NO response.

• Play around with different decisions to be made throughout the day and see how your body responds.

Day 4: Tweaking the Good and the Bad

• Find a neutral space where you can be super present and go through your itemized Best Day Ever list and get it into Alignment.

Day 5: Read, See, Verbalize, and Experience.

- Readout loud your Best Day Ever scenario so you can build those neural synapses in the full experience.

Day 6: When You're Not Feeling It
- Notice if your body or mind are experiencing any resistance, and if so, be curious to understand what the underlying cause could be.

Day 7: The Bigger Picture - Purpose
- Figure out what the underlying reason is that you have the goals and visions you are working towards.

Are you feeling any lighter than before?

WEEK FIVE – BRANCHES
CONNECTING YOU

The branches of a tree provide a veil of leaves that allows the tree to capture the sunlight. The branches continue in expansion outward to support the tree as it gets older and grows so that it can take in as much sun as possible. Sometimes trees will lean a little one way or another because they know their truth and must follow to where the sun shines most. The branches are also a vessel for bringing water and nutrients from the soil to the leaves. They are a connector to energy, and so are you.

This week you will venture out onto your branches and connect to your 'sun', for the energy and guidance that are your birthright. As you learn to go where the sun shines most for you, life will indeed get brighter for you. You will expand upon your knowledge and ultimately learn more about yourself and where you get to go next, in order to live a life of synchronistic flow.

After learning to listen to our bodies and understanding how to differentiate shifts between good and bad energies within – it's time to look outside of ourselves. Are you ready for more feedback? Time to take our awareness to another level, as we are going to start asking for guidance. Guidance comes from your subconscious, Universal energy, God, your soul, your gut, your angels, whatever you choose to believe will support you the most.

Each of the following days will introduce you to a new part of the alignment process, including relevant practices and activities to strengthen your intuition and offer reflective questions. The goals you have already written down, together with your existing resources, will support the connection with the guidance and items you will be asking for.

Day One: Awareness Styles

The first step in connecting with your awareness and Higher Beings, is understanding which method of communication works best for you. Developing these awareness capabilities is truly a gift and can take a tremendous amount of patience. Everyone can master at least one, if not more, of these styles of communication, commonly described as "channels". Your commitment to practicing the skills listed in the previous chapters will also support your journey here.

This week, take two or more days to explore these various methods. Take your time; don't rush through. Discover which is the most responsive within your body. If you have some concerns about these types of gifts, know that even the less aware person has probably experienced internal guidance and intuition on one level or another.

When surveyed, about 50% of people have mentioned that they have experienced some deeper channel of energy. Mainstream culture tries to discourage belief in these regularly occurring intuitive instances. Think about interactions with your "imaginary friends", as a child, or how sometimes you feel an instant connection with someone whom you've never met before. These are scenarios that people stumble upon, but don't delve deeper into, typically due to the fear of sounding crazy.

By now, within your body intelligence practice, it should be clear that coincidences and "crazy" interactions are simplified explanations for very complicated truths. Continue to exercise that trust! Let go of the negative energy and fear that might be holding you back from becoming more powerfully aligned.

Many don't recognize this type of energetic connection until a significant life event or trauma happens. A client of mine used to have reoccurring nightmares. She couldn't remember the last time she had slept through a peaceful eight hours. We had some conversations about it, and I shared that typically, energetic entities reach out to communicate with us around 3 a.m. Turns out that when she looked at the clock, most of the time, it was around that time. At first, she was nervous, but after over a year of minimal sleep, she was dying for change. She acknowledged that she felt like she already knew that they were reaching out to her. She was just embarrassed at the time to confide with me and scared to honor the truth because she didn't know what might open up for her once she did. Through study and practice, Lindsey became comfortable with her awareness of other entities and learned how to deal with her gifts, which allowed her to find peace and harmony during the night. She learned to connect and to have conversations with people who had passed on to other levels. It's been amazing to watch the transformation to her acknowledging that she was a medium.

Internal guidance abilities naturally occur throughout our lives, but taking up this journey means we want to control the power that we know is within us all. It takes time and practice to open oneself to what information is available and to find the best method to tap into these Sources of Truth.

My friend Lilly learned this lesson a few years ago. One day she randomly found herself half in and half out of sleep. She was attempting to take a nap, and out of nowhere, she received the message that her friend's uncle was going to die and was also told when it would happen. She was a little shocked by this situation and most definitely didn't feel like sharing the message. Sure enough, however, on that date, her friend's uncle became very ill and passed away.

While this may not be the message we would ever want to get for someone, it is a confirmation of our intuitive abilities. It's like the spirit world's way of getting our attention when we become more open and intentional on this level of consciousness. This concept is better known as ESP or extra-sensory perception. It also shows just how capable we are when we allow our bodies to receive information.

As Lilly slowly acknowledged this uncanny ability that she hadn't previously been aware of, she later tried to tap into it again, this time for a friend who had cancer. Lilly now knew she had a unique gift and decided to own it. This time there was a specific request: finding out the length of life left for her friend who had gotten a "3 months to live" diagnosis from the doctor. After meditating on the message, laying in bed, for what felt like hours, she finally received a message about how long her friend had to live.

Thankfully, it was much longer than the diagnosis, and fortunately, the news proved accurate. Lilly's situation is a great reminder not to give up on yourself too easily during this process of development. The more you trust yourself and are intentional about the progress of your awareness, the more impactful this gift can be in your life. Believing and practicing the art of guidance will make this easier through time. Be prepared to go at your own pace, and don't rush the process.

The more you can trust and connect with the spirit world, the faster these messages will flow because they are there ready for you to grasp. We can receive information through physical responses from the body. There are also additional ways of receiving messages and guidance, which we will discuss further. Everyone is different, and each particular approach can be further developed.

These days many refer to our internal compass as being aware, authentic, truthful, or woke to refer to being present and in-tune to guidance. Here are a few methods for you to see which one you relate to most. See if any stand out more than others, they may also correspond to what your style of learning is.

Clairvoyance

Clairvoyance is an overarching method for gaining insight and guidance about the future. There is some form of this innate ability within all people, but one must be intentional in developing this skill to see it manifest in their lives.

Clairvoyance can refer to the overall "psychic" abilities some intuitives are known for, yet explicitly it concerns visual messages. If you're experiencing dreams, chronic déjà vus, and visions that come true, keep a note of them! Have a particular dream journal. They may come in handy later for yourself or someone else.

I have had dreams during the night that come true the next day, regarding people I had only met once. And I'm the type of person who rarely remembers their dreams. It's worth paying attention, letting these small but mighty messages come through.

Clairaudience

Clairaudience is a mode of communication where one hears messages. These are messages that can be prophetic and provide insight into certain situations. If this is your gift, you must be careful to discern the difference between positive words that allow harmony, and those that are negative. Observe the difference by listening to your body; it knows!

Just the other day, I was out to dinner with one of my super in-tune friends, Jason. Mid-conversation, he put his hand up to stop us as a message was coming in that he wanted to hear. Next, he told me that "They" asked him to tell me that I needed to get specific and clear around some projects that I was working on. My question to him was "Who told you this?" This advice could be taken in a negative light, yet it's essential to know that the information is coming from the highest vibrational source. Jason didn't know which energies, beings, or angels he was getting his messages from. Regardless, it was still a useful input for me.

Another sign that you may have this gift is that you tend to hear a high pitch from time to time. If you have confirmed that it isn't linked to medical issues, this is your body's way of sensing a spiritual presence around you. The sound also could be the presence of your spiritual guide or other energies ready to be offering guidance.

Claircognizance

This ability and gift might be a bit harder to recognize and can prove quite interesting. If you are someone who happens to know things about people whom you've never met before, then you're probably claircognizant.

Before taking up the journey of being intuitive, you might have identified a natural sense of intuition that is usually spot on. It could be your guide giving you the information. At times it feels so natural that you may assume it is a reasonable thought process linked to paying attention to details.

If you find yourself in situations where you think you've met someone before, knowing that you never have, there's a good chance that claircognizance is your way of receiving intuitive signals. A friend of mine told me shortly after we met that he knows we were in contact in a past life. I was surprised by this comment at first. Yet, I did a little curious meditating, only to find out he had been an uncle of mine in a past life time! Some people have a special connection, and now I understand this means we knew each other from other lives.

Here's another example: my father was at an event decades ago where he felt an intense connection to one of the presenters, to the point where he couldn't ignore it. He thought that he had met her before, knowing factually that he never had. He ended up going to chat with her. They began a professional relationship that lasted over twenty-five years. After her passing, just shy of 97 years old, he was asked to be a board member of a design foundation promoting her legacy and contributions to the design world. She ended up being a tremendous inspiration to him during his career.

Be in a state of curiosity when you have the feeling of connection - you never know where the relationship could take you. By the way, a connection does not necessarily imply a romantic one. However, we often hear people say about their partner "I just knew he was the one". Why did they know?

Claircognizant people must initially gain an understanding of the difference between the gift at work and an acute sense of observation. For instance, if you ever take the Meyers-Briggs personality test, your results might show "strategic" as one of your characteristics. Those with this trait can generally take in their surroundings and assess them quickly. It is an instinctual part of their personality. It doesn't always mean that the information is accurate. Information we observe filters through our personal biases, experiences, and subconscious thoughts that we might not even admit to ourselves. The internal learning traits are very different from using claircognizance to receive external information.

It's a good idea to assess your learning traits before diving into this skill. The better you know yourself, the easier it will be to decide which messages or guidance are of claircognizance nature. Build awareness of when you are consciously thinking of something, and when a random observation comes to mind. Information regarding considerations that you weren't thinking about can be messages from guides offering you guidance.

Clairsentience

Clairsentience is the gift of receiving information through feelings. Introverts tend to identify with this one the most.

Toddlers, before the age of four, are especially sensitive to the vibrations and people in their environment.

One day, as I was talking on the phone to my best friend, I received an incoming call from someone named Victoria, whom I "ignored". My friend's three-year-old daughter, Samantha, who was in the car during our conversation, started yelling from the back seat "Victoria, Victoria!" I was in awe, as I had not said the name out loud, and I was talking to my friend from the other side of the country! My friend then confessed that things like this had been happening a lot with her daughter.

I then decided to test Samantha and started asking her questions that I was curious about. Surprisingly, she gave me accurate and insightful responses that added clarity to the situation. She was only three! An age when children are barely making out sentences! Children genuinely are "wise beyond their years", they don't have past stories stockpiled in their subconscious to divert judgment. Kids are much more receptive and open to the guidance that surrounds us all. Feel free to entertain yourself and ask serious life questions to young children to see what their response is. If anything, it will be fun!

Now that we've gone through the different types of awareness and modes of communication, ask yourself these questions:

Did any of them stand out when you thought about past synchronistic situations?

Did your body elicit a response as you read about it?

Did you experience a warm and fuzzy feeling or a tingling sensation?

Keep paying attention to your body's reactions. It's ok if you haven't "heard" anything yet, the time will come, and this is not a part of the alignment journey to take lightly. It takes lots of patience to understand how these types of awareness styles play out in your life.

Day Two: Follow Your Instinct

It is important to acknowledge who you are connecting with, as there are many choices! This also depends on your personal beliefs. One view affirms that higher powers and divine beings have a resonating presence with you. Then there are other spiritual beings, such as spirit guides and various levels of angels. The last Beings that you can't forget is the spiritual version of yourself, your soul, or higher self, as well as your inner child.

We will go through some of the sources of guidance in the next section, but for now, I encourage you to do a self-check-in. As you read the following sources of messages and advice, see if one immediately resonates with you, without doing any further research.

Identify one spiritual being to explore: God, the Universe, Gaia (Mother Earth), highly vibrating spirit guides, your higher self or inner child.

From here, play around with the form of communication sources you have chosen. No one can tell you which is the best for you to connect to, but those connections will affect the future of your development in awareness and getting aligned.

Always keep in mind what goals you are looking to achieve by becoming a more aligned person. If you are feeling a sense of loneliness and wandering within yourself, then connecting to something bigger than you may be the best place to start. For example, those working to heal from their past may want to move forward with their higher self or inner child.

Developing the skill of discernment by listening to your body, the understanding of good and destructive spirits, is crucial. Make sure you are only receiving messages from positive and harmonious beings who will help you and others. Feel free to triple-check yourself by figuring out if situations are a YES or NO for you, as previously explained.

Day Three: Discover Your Mentor(s)

As we open up to our sensitivity, our journey is getting more exciting each day. Continue being open during this section. Some of this may be uncomfortable, and if that's the case, then it might not be right for you; trust your gut. I encourage you to trust your body, not your head. Your head may limit you and guide you away because of upbringing and stories that project onto you, instead of you coming to know your truth. My goal is to get you out of your head, remove analysis paralysis, and be present with your body. Remember, this process is YOUR journey -not someone else's. Do it for you. The goal is to develop a relationship with internal and external communication so powerfully that you know you are taken care of. Life as you know it is about to get smoother and more joyous! Do what feels right and know the Universe has your back.

God, the Universe, & Truth

I have combined God, the Universe, and Truth as interchangeable "titles", allowing you the freedom to honor what feels the most natural to you. You may believe, for example, in God as the highest power and the ultimate controller and creator of the Universe. If you believe that a Being is active in the process, then this will be the most highly recommended resource for guidance, your choice.

When my emotions and vibrations are feeling a little off, I choose to go to God. Prayer is the most common way people connect. It is different from meditation because it is more of a dialogue that we're seeking between the Higher Power and ourselves. Prayers can be answered, and valuable lessons learned as a result of these conversations. Moments of reflection on these conversations can happen through meditation, yet guidance from this experience is most beneficial when these two practices, dialogue and reflection, coincide.

We all have our definitions, and this is mine. See if it is something that resonates. When I connect to God / the Universe, I see them as the motherboard of a computer. God is the controller who connects everything. Without the Universe, I wouldn't exist, and without me, there wouldn't be a Universe for me to experience. We are one and the same, and God lives within us.

We need each other to operate. The Universe is the operating system for life-force to manifest and allow us to do some programming so that we can work in unison. The more you understand yourself and grow a deeper awareness of these energies, the more you will be able to create a life that works in harmony. Think of your life as needing compatible software to operate on the Universe's system; otherwise, you might be an Apple iOS system trying to run Android software, and that doesn't work. That would be living a life in dis-harmony, possibly from a victim stance, living in reaction mode instead of coming from a space of creation. "Updating" your software versions regularly, throughout life, allows you to stay in ownership of the journey you are creating.

For some, this comparison might be a little out of sorts. The description is necessary to understand that God is here for you to work with, play with, and create from. Have fun. Life is a game, a playground to learn lessons and strategize your next move. When you treat living as such, life will be taken more lightly, preventing you from having dramatic and emotional mood swings.

Here's an example of shifting up any lull energy situations and having fun with it. Let's say I'm about to go to an event, and I'm feeling a little under the weather. The last thing I want to do is bring my low energy into a room of people and meet them in this manner. My goal is always to bring people joy; it's my thing. When I come from an understanding that God is here to work with me, yet also the controller of the Universe, I want to connect to Him and ask Him to "download" or "update" me with the feelings of joy and love where I can share this energy and upgraded vibration with those around me. And since bringing joy to others is very much in alignment with my being, the "downloads" happen effortlessly.

Through prayer and intention, I work with God to program my "software" so that my life is more compatible and shifts smoothly with the changes in my immediate environments. It takes two to tango, and through mutual connection and prayer requests, I see results.

However, if you are asking for something that goes against your personal integrity, you will most likely not see the results you are after, or at least not with ease.

Let's bring in Bible talk. Raised Catholic, I now practice as a non-denominational Christian as long as it aligns with my truth. This statement might rub you the wrong way, and I ask your body: Is that judgment coming from your head or your heart? Is it from your upbringing, from something someone told you, or is it your truth? If you are familiar with the Bible, you know that I have been taught about surrendering to what God has in store for me. Personally, I'm not 100% aligned to that statement, as there are two parties involved, God and I. It's not necessarily surrendering, rather a conscious removing of expectations.

When someone comes to me and says ' I don't know what is next for me, I don't know what I should do next with my life', I ask: 'What do YOU want next in your life? What do YOU choose?' This is a much stronger place to come from, and if we are to co-create, we'd better have some thoughts about it.

You might be familiar with the verse from Matthew 7:7 "Ask, and you shall receive." My understanding of the verse is that while submitting our intentions, prayers, and requests, we open ourselves to the possibilities of working in partnership with God. Only after our stating our requests can we surrender to being led towards those goals and desires. Again, they must be in alignment with your highest and best potential, and might not always end up the way you think they should.

Higher Self

You are driven by internal guidance. The Higher Self is in complete alignment with your vision and dreams on a deeper level. The Higher Self sees deeper connections to others in our lives and paths to our goals.

Think of it as having a chess game with the perfect strategy to win. Although it's always altered depending on the other player's moves, there is a sure way to win.

At the moment, I'm coaching multiple clients, writing this book, and doing strategy consulting for clients, along with real estate. It can get overwhelming to pick the correct priority to be intentional towards and figure out which activity is of utmost priority for me. When sensing this confusion, I pause and connect to my Higher Self and ask which path is best for me to work on, that particular moment or day, and the most aligned to my Best Day Ever. As long as I have a strong sense of trust, acknowledging that my Higher Self is in perfect alignment with my goals, I know that I'm guided towards the ideal path.

Inner Child

Our inner child loves to connect, be entertained, pull our strings, and play jokes on us. It is also where our guilty pleasures come from and help us feel relaxed. Those little things that seem small, but make things better — or sometimes more annoying — come from the spark of innocence that is a significant driver in our daily decisions.

Sometimes children will frustrate you, yet know that they are here to support your awareness. The beauty of the inner child is that they help with your present and future while observing the past. When you are noticing recurring themes, dive into them, and find ways to work with your inner child to resolve them. I do not have children of my own yet, but everyone knows that children will start acting out if they feel ignored. They can shed light on places you could look within more deeply. You may not have known that paying attention to them not only helps with your guidance; their distractions support managing daily stressors as well.

One of my friends is constantly going through the craziest situations, life-threatening car accidents, and scenarios that I thought would only happened in movies. Through the years, I have noticed a pattern. I asked if she had noticed that these experiences tended to occur around the holidays. It turns out that almost every Christmas in her youth, her parents were in jail, or she was in the hospital. She had virtually no recollection of a time when the holiday season brought her joy.

From a coaching standpoint, I would invite her to connect to her inner child, who has kept this traumatic theme going into adulthood. She could meditate and see how she could appease her three-year-old self, thus making her feel safe, protected, and loved so that heading into future holidays, she would experience the joy and love that she deserves. Through digging, she might find out that her inner child doesn't know what it feels like to be safe and secure around the holidays because she is often alone during that period. After getting to the root of this story, I would recommend she provide an experience that might reframe feelings for her inner child so that she begins to feel this much-needed safety through the holiday season. She could probe into what request she might need to fill the void creating these ordeals every year.

One solution could be joining a stable community, a group of friends, or a church-like environment throughout the year. During the holidays, when many of her friends leave for their families, she would never feel alone because she would have a group or community she'd be part of. She would then create another version of a connected family, one that has a better track record than her original family, and which her inner child can trust.

Another way to access the inner child is through doodling. Soon you'll hear about a lost camera story from childhood that I solved through doodling. Sometimes I draw something in my journal, and it's fascinating to see what follows from my body when I tap into that part of me.

Other Spiritual Guides and Beings

Other spiritual guides aren't controllers like the Universe or God; they are more connected to the divine energy source than our subconscious selves. These beings can take on various forms. Your choice in seeking out these beings is up to you, figure out whether it aligns to your truth or not.

Keep in mind the saging and clearing practices we mentioned at the beginning of the book, aimed at removing the negative and lower vibration frequencies. Only seek beings possessing the highest forms of truth and light. Embrace their energies when interacting with them, encouraging only positive high vibrating interaction. It also may be a good idea to consult a mentor when seeking other spiritual beings, as mentors can help guide you towards positive Beings of light and harmony. Again, discuss with your temple body what is true for you.

I used to work with spirit guides such as Jesus and others. Some guides are assigned to us pre-birth, others come in and out of our lives, or take on shifts. They could also be spirits of the trees or of water. Some people lump them in with angels. Just the other day, I was meditating for a client, which I typically do before working with them. She's not a God person, so I asked during the meditation if there was anyone else I should consult for her, and I received the message "the Ocean". This message couldn't have been more perfect as my client would be a marine biologist, if she had to live her life again. That's how much she loves the water.

It doesn't matter who you choose to engage with for guidance, as long as you wholeheartedly believe that it's the highest vibrational energy possible. This process allows you to work with other levels of your brain, which is of utmost importance.

I have even tried asking people who have passed away for guidance. Once I decided to consult with Steve Jobs on a startup idea, and the advice I got out of this session was astonishing. His direction was solid yet harsh, and I couldn't have thought it up myself. However, it was a little too strenuous as I was the only person working on the project; it didn't feel in alignment, so I didn't move forward with his thoughts.

In *Think and Grow Rich*, Napoleon Hill discusses having nightly Imaginary Council meetings with people such as Ralph Waldo Emerson, Thomas Edison, Abraham Lincoln, Andrew Carnegie, and Henry Ford. These meetings brought creative inspiration and clarity. Hill describes this opportunity through the sixth sense and considers it under the Laws of Nature.

Some people like to use the question 'What Would Jesus Do?' These questions open your thought process for a different view. It's a simple trick to get out of our heads.

I heard from some speakers that they channel the energy of other powerful speakers before getting on stage. Even if you don't believe that you're getting guidance from someone like Steve Jobs, your mind can easily alter to his similar mindset to pull this guidance for you, so it doesn't matter if you believe that it is actually happening or not. Should you decide to try this method, you will receive a uniquely fresh new perspective.

Messages or guidance are motivators to lead intentional lives and develop a stronger intuition so you can understand when various spirits may be at work. For some, naturally, knowing that spirits are always surrounding them provides the needed comfort. Once I grasped this concept of spirits surrounding me, I felt so much grace in my life.

I started opening up to the spirits and involving them in my life around the same time that I moved to Venice Beach, California, from Portland, Oregon. Compared to Portland,

Venice Beach brought a lot of discomfort, with people on drugs or mentally ill walking the streets, yelling random profanities. Walking anywhere at night was extremely uncomfortable. Knowing that there were angels and spirits everywhere, even in the grass, trees, and flowers, carried such a strong sense of serenity and protection for me. Understanding that these energies, spirits, and angels were on the look-out provided a sense of safety.

Focusing on which specific guide you are working with is not necessary unless this is something you want to dive into on your journey. The guides are here to offer service, protection, and love.

Another thing to remember when working with guides is that they are not of this Earthly time frame. This means that you must ask your questions or request support in the present moment.

Archangels

Archangels are considered God's chief messengers, here for your guidance and support. You can choose to work with archangels individually, or angels, below. Think of a work-flow organizational chart.

GOD

↓

ARCHANGELS

↓

MINISTRY OF ANGELS

↓

HUMAN BEINGS

Some feel that we can't go directly from Human beings to God or archangels, yet I completely disagree with that.

Each archangel has his specialty, so you may want to go to them or pray to them for specific requests. When I work with archangels, I find that I receive more comprehensive advice instead of particular steps or instructions for accomplishing a targeted result. Every person will receive different outcomes when reaching out to archangels. Here's a quick summary of the archangels and their specialty areas for guidance, although there are more archangels than those presented below for you to go to, should you choose.

Archangel Michael: For energy, protection, and forward movement when you are feeling sluggish.

Archangel Gabriel: For peace, when experiencing anxiety and stress or other overwhelming emotions.

Archangel Raphael: For reviving your entire body and spirit.

Archangel Uriel: For action steps that move you forward, although only one step is delivered at a time.

Archangel Sariel: For coordination, organization, planning, and systems.

Archangel Raziel: For the cultivation of new ideas and recognition of self-power.

A while ago, I decided to turn to Archangel Uriel after reviewing a session of archangel cards with Doreen Virtue. I find value in them, and still go to them on rare occasions. Angel cards are like Tarot cards or other advice decks in that you pull random cards from a deck to see what messages you receive. When I drew Archangel Uriel's card, the message was that Uriel only delivers one step of advice each day, so I started reaching out regularly to ask for the most impactful advice of the day. Each piece of information I received was simple yet profound, with powerful ripple effects.

I'd ask: *"What one piece of impactful advice do you have for me that will allow me to achieve my dreams?"*

A: *"You already are an open human being, now start allowing that which you desire to stick with you."*

A: *"Fuel yourself up on love before sharing with others."*

A: *"Take a moment to recognize your past accomplishments."*

A: *"Don't hide; be seen."*

These powerful messages aren't always the easiest to remember, so I started a notecard collection. It makes it easier for me to thumb through and randomly pick reminders, knowing that I am on a very intentional mission with my life.

In this practice, make sure you are connecting to the highest divine source and grounded intentionally, before proceeding. I go to my Archangel cards when I feel the desire for support outside of my usual techniques and only when it feels in alignment with me.

Ministry of Angels

The Ministry of angels provides comforting support for me. They are the collective of angels who are messengers for us, and many also consider them spirit guides and guardian angels, as they are the closest to humanity. This scenario is one I use regularly. Have you ever jumped into your car, started driving, and felt a little frazzled, maybe from things that have happened earlier in the day? Or perhaps it's the holiday season, and everyone seems a bit on edge, and accidents are happening left and right?

Almost every time I get in the car now, I immediately pray to the Ministry of Angels for protection and support. I ask for a ball of white light to be placed around my vehicle to ensure that I safely get to my destination and on time. Their primary charge is to protect us from harm, and many people from various backgrounds call upon angels for safety.

Another way I use the Ministry of angels is to reach my goals, for example, attracting clients. I'll describe the individual and ask for their support in bringing them my way.

About a year ago, I had a property that I needed to find a tenant for because the previous tenant decided to cut the lease early. It was in the middle of winter and the middle of the month as well, obviously a terrible time to find a new tenant quickly. I specifically requested the Ministry to help me find a new tenant who needed a place immediately. I also asked the Ministry of angels for someone who would love my place as much as I did, so that they would bring good energy and love into the home. Then I let it go and allowed the angels to take over. Within 24 hours, I received a message from someone who had just moved from California to Oregon and needed a place ASAP. It's a little like magic, but more about specificity with your request and faith. When working with any spiritual being, you must be clear and concise to get your point across.

Requests, in general, are pretty similar. You must define your desires, fully submit to your intentions, and trust that you are being taken care of. Building trust and keeping faith can be the hardest part of all. The angels need your trust and gratitude to do their best work. Similarly to micromanagement, when we get attached to how our employees or children do things, they tend to act and perform worse. It appears that we don't trust them to create the desired results, and this tense energy transfers to them as we regularly check on their progress.

Day Four: Questions

By now, you've developed active listening skills to understand your body and possibly an openness to outside energetic guidance. Today, we will put these skills to work and connect with the external sources and high vibrational energies. These spiritual sources become your support system. The beauty is connecting with the spiritual helpers who are in alignment with you. They will support streamlining your path towards alignment with your specific goals and Best Day Ever.

At first, it can be scary to connect to 'the sixth sense'. However, the intention is to reach the highest frequency of spiritual sources. You want to encourage an increased personal vibration that you radiate to those around you.

As you increase your positive vibrations and personal energy, you'll get what you want, and faster, as long as it is in your best interest. Over the next couple of days, we'll dive into gaining a better understanding of what types of questions can help you progress in your alignment journey and find where these answers rest. The process is pretty exciting, and once you get the hang of it, I'm confident you'll be using these tools for the rest of your life.

These methods will be useful for life. When I first started, I think I was doing it multiple times a day. We are going to go down a few layers because it's time for you to remove all that might hinder you.

Now, before going further, I want you to know my definition of success: being joyful in the present moment. When you get out of your head, become available to the presence and grateful for all that is, nothing feels better. You will no longer be wondering what's going to happen in the future, or why something has happened in the past. Presence is a new state of mind. It is fully submerged in the now.

Personally, I choose not to connect to any other sources until I experience a connection to God, as this solidifies a knowing that I'm united to the highest vibration possible before receiving additional input from others.

Strengthening our connections with our surroundings can reveal answers to our deepest desires and burning questions, as long as we're asking the best questions for ourselves. Take some time today to discover barriers and blocks within. For example, some of our most superficial questions – about the clothes we wear, new car we choose, a hobby or dinner plans with an old friend – can stem from the ego vs. a subconscious desire that's longing to be addressed.

Know that you also have the right to question whatever you like. I encourage you to work towards achieving the goal that will be creating the most impact. When asking about the future, should you receive any information, know that future guidance is purely there for your acceptance or for you to make a change, and it can quickly shift based on your knowledge of the scenario. Similarly, when asking about the past, your guidance will be about learning the lessons so that you can move past them. When asking questions, you may feel swayed one way or another. If you feel this way, it's true. When I experience a pull that doesn't feel authentic, I pause for a moment and state,

"I surrender to truth. I surrender my ego."

The ground work of stating can makes a huge difference.   I love to ask questions about things that are frustrating to me because I know that when I'm frustrated I am not in alignment with my best life and not listening to the body intelligence available to me. Sometimes, when I ask questions, I get an answer right away. I may also receive answers randomly throughout the day or the next day. Trust you'll have the answers delivered to you.

In my real estate career, once in a while, I encounter complications around selling a particular home or dealing with a client. So I sit quietly and ask:

Where can I go next to get this home sold?

What have I not done yet to get this home sold?

Is there something the seller needs to do?

I have gained some creative insight for my clients through my meditations, asking these questions.

On a personal level, I became aware of my biggest 'walls' when I was single and actively dating. I need to spend time meditating or journaling, asking questions about people I go on dates with and whether or not I should continue to date them. During dates with guys, I found myself getting into a lot of judgment, which always drives me nuts. I aspire to step out of judgment and into my heart, to get clear on connection, values, and more. Regarding relationships, many of my answers have come to me during twenty-minute power naps, because this is a time when my mind becomes relaxed yet remains slightly conscious, knowing I'll be up again soon.

Looking back, you can even ask why you haven't met specific goals. You might get answers such as 'You are to achieve a lesson' or 'It is coming, be patient.' Don't hesitate to ask a follow-up question right after you receive an answer.

Notice yourself throughout the day, thinking about something that frustrates you, or thinking/saying something negative. Stop yourself at that moment, maybe jot down thoughts so that you can come back to them later and figure out a new perspective or a solution. This will support you in getting out of the negative thought patterns and closer to joy in the present moment.

Question examples:

Is now the best time to request a meeting with management for a position I'd like to create?

Is it in my highest and best interest to continue dating _____?

Is it in my highest and best interest to hire _____ as an employee on our team?

Is it in my highest and best interest to start my day with exercise, or exercise later tonight?

Is now the best time to conceive a child?

Go into this practice without expectations and listen to what your soul is trying to share with you. You can even treat this as if you were using one of those toy "Magic 8 Balls" from your childhood to answer your questions. Feel free to jot them down in your journal or in a voice memo.

Use practices from previous chapters for listening to your body and properly exploring experiences and feelings through meditation. An excellent advantage of increasing your internal awareness is getting to understand your personal power and how you connect to the rest of the Universe. This opportunity is part of the human condition, part of being self-sufficient. Being truly in-tune with your truth allows for great things to be accomplished during your lifetime, along with your universal support system. Using a system that's available to you will open your ability to reach the potential you seek and desire.

Living in curiosity all day, I have tons of questions. One of my friends used to say that I had a cartoon style "thought bubble" above me at all times. When making decisions and listening to my body, I sometimes decide I'd like additional external assistance from guiding sources. Extra support, such as recommendations from friends, is filtered by their stories and subjective judgment.

As you listen to your body, you may notice how it is affected by particular places and scenarios. Asking the right questions can help you understand your surroundings and create the change and security you're seeking.

Keep these questions somewhere safe and play with them over the next few days. You'll discover which questions work for you, how to form them, which method of communication is best for you, and how to reconsider and reformulate the questions later on. Also, when you get an answer, don't hesitate to ask the question in multiple ways to see if the answer changes at all.

Day Five: Connection

Your method will evolve as you become more aware and present to the guidance you are receiving. For example, with this book, I started by handwriting, as that was the easiest for me to channel and download. Then I moved on to this quiet space overlooking the marina, which became my personal "cathedral", where I could fully relax and type on my laptop. At this moment, I have now graduated to dictating the book. It all becomes more comfortable with practice!

My favorite style is still journaling; however, about a year ago, one of my friends encouraged me to stop writing everything as it stops me from being present to the guidance coming right into my mind. She is so right! Even when working with clients, I always wanted to do phone sessions because that way, I could be in my quiet place, without distractions, which would allow additional guidance and visions to come through effortlessly. Through the push of some clients, I eventually "graduated" to in-person sessions, being present to my thoughts and guidance.

My original method started something like this:

Dear Spirit Guides of the Highest Truth and Light,
I'm having this _____ problem and am looking for your heavenly guidance to support me in working through it. What do you suggest?

Then I would wait until I felt an urge in my hand or nudge in my heart to start putting pen to paper. When I first started, I was so in my head, waiting for the moment to arrive, that sometimes nothing would happen. I was putting so much pressure on the result. Then I moved on to doodling, such as drawing circles on top of the page, until I felt the urge to write. Sometimes it would take seconds. Other times it would take ten minutes.

I also noticed that the more detailed my question, the easier it was for me to receive answers. You can play around with various ways of asking the questions to see what works best for you. Now, when I ask questions, I am so connected and in tune, that answers almost always come instantly.

Another way to ask questions is to do it right before you go to bed. You may wake up in the middle of the night or in the morning with an answer. I often inform clients who are having trouble connecting to an answer that they are yearning; this might be their avenue because they are relaxed while sleeping. Of course, there's always silent meditation as well, asking a question while sitting up straight with your spine erect to allow the guidance to come in with ease.

If I don't receive an instant answer when I ask questions, I get to work on my presence with silent meditations to get back in the flow. Sometimes I'll even get woken up around 3:30 a.m. Typically, I'll resist the awakening because I want to sleep, yet when I do, it will happen again and again the following mornings until I listen to the wakening guidance.

Another form of meditation is through movement, so maybe ask the question before you go to a yoga class or on a run or walk, to see what comes to you throughout the activity. Remember how my emotions finally broke through when I did Bikram yoga for thirty days? That was mostly peeling back the layers, breaking down boundaries and walls and getting deep within.

Many writers and artists do their best work late at night. There is less effort to tap into your subconscious when the melatonin starts being produced, while the sun goes down. Melatonin allows your mind to relax, which is also a process of becoming less alert.

Personally, I prefer to ask my questions first thing in the morning. It's my way of starting the day, feeling refreshed and excited about whatever I learn through the answers for that day.

You can also try asking questions throughout the day to see which time of the day resonates best for you. You may find that during the evening you are too exhausted, so guidance comes more efficiently in the morning. Play around!

You can even ask the same question to different guides or divinities to see how they align with you for this particular process. The method is similar to bringing up the situation to multiple friends and having them all say something different. Your imagination is powerful; it will support you tremendously during this week and forever!

Day Six: Practice Patience

Dive into how other cultures are connecting with their guides. Ask your friends if they are open to, aware of, or already have spiritual communication and guidance.

My friend's friend, Melody, was in a youth Bible study group, and everyone made fun of her method of prayer. Melody told them that she didn't like to pray before going to bed because she could never really focus and would just fall asleep. So she prayed in the shower, and her version of saying the prayer was singing songs of requests. To her, it felt more natural to sing her prayers as they would rise over the noise of the day. It worked for her – plus, it sounded like a lot more fun. Keep this in mind when you're connecting. Transcendence isn't some chore. It is a fun, joyous, enlightening way to give more purpose to your lives and goals.

Have fun with this exercise, be light-hearted and deliberate, as too much pressure can keep your answers at bay. You might need to practice specific parts of this week's topics for more days than the action plan suggests. Go at your own pace, stay true to your needs, and do not succumb to procrastination. Own it and sit with the knowledge that you will receive answers, even when it might seem difficult or you feel like you're not being heard.

It took me years to get to the point where I am now, and I'm still learning and evolving with the practice. Sometimes my head seems to be a bit foggier; however, the answers always come. You can even be transparent in your communication with the spirit guides. Don't be afraid to tell them:

"I am feeling a little resistant at this moment, please support me in breaking down any walls as I desire to connect with you and receive your advice."

After all, the purpose of this connection is to allow yourself to be vulnerable and open. Although I have been giving you specific guidelines, this book is meant for you to make it your own. For example, the other day, I was writing down my intentions for the New Year. I threw them into a flame to be carried into the Universe, while the person I was with couldn't stand the idea of throwing her intentions into the fire. To her, that would have meant something different, such as burning them away with disregard. A perfect example that we must always act upon what is right for our individual views and personal integrity.

What works best for me doesn't always work for my clients. We learn through the presence of our body's elicited responses and fine-tuning - which may take a lifetime to achieve. Even after years of practicing, working with my intuition, God, the spirit guides, and angels, I still change things up every three months. Communication is a journey. As long as you are building upon the foundation, you will guide yourself towards the best and highest ways of creating magical results for yourself.

Divine beings are here to serve you. They are waiting for you to work with them. Here is a suggested plan of how you can break up this week. Feel free to take as many days for each step as you feel you need. It can take time getting comfortable communicating with these higher beings and your inner child. Being patient and keeping the faith are the keys to success this week.

Day Seven: Take Action

Once you become comfortable and figure out your groove, you can start going back and forth with questions and answers, like a normal conversation. Don't be nervous; your guides want to help you! They get excited when you listen to them and use the information they give you. Don't take it for granted; make sure to express gratitude at the end of every conversation.

When you ignore the guidance, you ignore the gifts and blessings brought your way, so you may start to create a drought in further communication, until restored. Guides are always ready to support you, and they want acknowledgment for doing so, just as you would in helping others.

How many times will you invite a friend out who seems to be lonely, if they always say 'No, thank you'? Eventually, you stop the invitations as they were not receptive to your support.

Your life can be full and abundant in every way. Designing this type of environment requires you to be grateful for your current situation, thankful for learning the lessons in this book, appreciative of the problems that you face because you know that you are learning something that will support you in getting to the next level. Through joy and gratitude, along with presence to that divine guidance coming your way, allow yourself to break through to the next chapter of your life.

Use the Best Day Ever exercise daily as a grounding point for asking questions. You can ask how to set up your day, what to prioritize. I also use questions to come up with additional action steps towards my goals. Sometimes I do this just once a week, on Sundays, to set up the week, and other times I'm a little needier and ask for direction daily.

These are just a few questions to get you started:

What's most vital for you to tackle next?

What action step would create the most momentum towards your Best Day Ever?

Who should you talk to in order to get to that next level?

Get creative and curious with your questioning and use it to your advantage, towards aligned actions.

SUMMARY - BRANCHES

Day 1: Awareness Styles

• Put the key methods into practice for a few days, and reflect on which one you're most comfortable with. Considering you're experienced with guidance, this may be an opportunity to strengthen a different method.

Day 2: Follow Your Instinct

• Does something already stand out to you? Play with it before researching to see what comes naturally, aside from my suggestions.

Day 3: Discover Your Mentor(s)

• Research which guide would be best to answer your questions. Explore who you feel most comfortable asking guidance from. Take this step very seriously. It may be useful to write down why this particular guide is sticking out to you. You may find more questions in the process, which usually means you're on the right track.

• Know, this isn't a quick turn around, don't get discouraged. It can take time to find which source you'll work with, who you feel most connected to, and of the highest vibrating awareness available for you.

Day 4: Questions

• What questions matter to you at this time? Figure out the priority order of questions that have an impact in getting you aligned now in your life.

Day 5: Connection

• Take what you have learned in the previous week and start asking your questions, noticing what time of the day works best for you.

Day 6: Practice Patience

• Offer Prayer, gratitude, and your intention to develop a regular practice of communication through the various channels of communication you've explored. The intention must be specific and genuine, and you must request to only work with Beings of the highest light and vibrations. It's crucial to be specific about who you are communicating with to get results of harmony and happiness.

Day 7: Take Action

• Get in the habit of asking questions in the morning or at the start of your week to figure out your highest and best game plan for accomplishing your Best Day Ever.

What is the biggest

takeaway you've

learned about yourself

this past week?

WEEK SIX – LEAVES & SEEDS
MANIFESTING

Every part of the tree is essential to its functioning and its whole existence. The leaves support the tree with photosynthesis; without light, the tree will die. The leaves foster the exchange of energy, bringing vital nutrients to the tree, and when the time comes, letting go and releasing, allowing for new growth to form in upcoming months. Then you have the wondrous seeds which grow in their fruit with the full intention of rebirth.

How powerful it is to fully know your mission; the tree is a magnificent example of alignment, and you also deserve to understand your mission and find alignment. This week will support you in fully taking in the light and guidance while planting your seeds to bring forth your dreams and goals. You have a compelling vision to communicate to the Universe, so let's pave the way to allow it to manifest.

Virtualize: Using all our senses to manifest what we want.

You have found a vision that is aligned to you, you've tweaked it, so it feels just right. Now let's take it a few notches deeper because you may have been having this vision for the longest time, but it hasn't manifested just yet!

My next questions to you are:

Are you feeling giddy about your vision?

Is it exciting for you at all?

It is time to manifest these goals creating results, in clarity with an openness to receive. If you're not open, little progress will be made, keeping you on the same track as before. Get out of that vicious circle; it's time to step forward into new territory as this is where up-leveling your life begins, in the space of something outside the ordinary.

You may be thinking- I've done this manifesting, law of attraction stuff before and it doesn't work!' You're not the first one. There are other things that most people don't take into consideration when using visualization to manifest their dreams. I emphasize alignment via body intelligence, as it includes it all, energy, consciousness, subconscious, senses, sometimes even what you're eating as well!

For manifesting and attracting, we've got to go deeper inward and peel away those layers. Often times we have a breakthrough or an a-ha! moment, and then, a day or a week later, we understand that there is a whole new level to dive deep into. Know that the more inner work you do, the more external goals will manifest, effortlessly. The deeper down you go, the more expanded those vibrational levels become. Hence, aligned action.

Day One: Our Individual Patterns - Past Goals

Get your journal and write down the dreams and goals that you have been trying to accomplish for years and have not succeeded. Maybe some of them were already tweaked during your Best Day Ever exercise?

Maybe those unaccomplished goals were not in alignment with your body. Think about it.

Did you actively choose to take steps towards your goals, daily?

Did you decide it was too difficult to carry out the goals, taking a more leisurely route?

Did life "happen" to get in the way?

Reality will always interrupt if you let it be an excuse. Random experiences happen all the time, but it all depends on how you look at it. Here's where a coach or friend can come in extremely handy, as they will keep you accountable.

For example, let's say you've just decided to lose ten pounds in the next two months. You wake up, eat healthily, and you get your workout in. Then when you get to work, your boss gives you a new project that will take up the majority of your time for the next month or so. The following day, you are already feeling worn down a bit because of this new project. The extra stress is a heavy weight on your shoulders, and you don't make it to the gym and then get frustrated by your lack of commitment to your self.

You can be sure that every time you are about to make a transition in your life, something is going to pop up to try and get in the way. Every time I signed up for a personal development workshop, something came up, making me not want to go. For example, my dog once got sick and needed a $5000 surgery, about two weeks after I had committed to a three-month leadership course. Many things were popping up that told me not to do it, including a new relationship budding and other things that were pulling me in a completely different direction as soon as I signed up.

I decided to go through with the leadership course anyway and figured out a solution to have everything work in my favor. My dog was going to be okay; he was already thirteen years old, and surgery was riskier than allowing him to live the rest of life. At the heightened moment, though, I was very nervous, feeling like these were all signs for me to do something different.

I have continued to notice this interruptive trend almost every time I was about to do something big. When participating in half Ironman triathlons, the week before each race, I would get sick, sprain an ankle or something work-related would try and pull me away from accomplishing my triathlon the following weekend. Still, I always finished the race. I "simply" pushed through the obstacles that popped up and re-framed what was going on that seemed to be a setback and shift it in my mind to something that served me moving forward.

Whichever way you decide to go will work out for that choice, there is no right or wrong. At least you have an alignment process to follow, by listening to your body, no more needing to get emotionally worked up about decisions!

The next time something pops up and tries to stop you from moving forward with your goals, take a moment, and decide not to let it interfere. Sometimes this simple decision is enough to change the course of events. Another approach is to become aware of how this supposed obstacle is supporting you in your dreams through re-framing. If you were to share with a good friend who supports your goals or a coach, would they see your challenge as something that helps you? Sometimes it is worth talking to someone else to get a second perspective on the situation because it can be difficult at times to get out of our heads.

What other things have stopped you from moving forward? When you shed light by uncovering these trends and patterns, the clarity alone could push you to the next level. You get to accomplish your goals, don't let anything get in the way this time!

Think about the goals you wrote down in Week 5, before the Alignment process. You could also think about other dreams and goals from your past. They could even be from fifteen years ago. Take a moment to think about the things that you wanted and never accomplished. Allow yourself to spend some time and meditate on this and see what bubbles up. Once you have come up with some of these goals, you'll learn to assess them.

Why weren't they a possibility for you?

What obstacles were in the way?

Are any of the reasons part of the victim mentality discussed in Week Two?

The goal is to move beyond these unaccomplished goals. Analyze these unfulfilled dreams and see what comes up for you. It could be a story from childhood that has created a block, or it could be the people you surround yourself with. Subconscious blocks stemming from our past may limit us in everyday life, causing us to have walls, and we will be discussing this shortly.

In my case, a personal example could be that gifts and money are taken away from me as soon as I receive them. Subconscious programming is common. I see it for private clients and real estate clients, as well. For example, I had a good-sized commission from closing in real estate, and then, all of a sudden, my home needed a new roof, which ate up most of that income.

When I meditated on this trend in my life, a story from when I was three years old popped up. I remember getting a cool camera, and being excited about it and then losing it, that same day, in an ivy patch in the side yard. I remember it was dusk, and I was frantically searching through the ivy trying to find the camera, yet I never did. I probably searched for that camera daily whenever I went outside. From this experience, I made up a story that cemented itself in my subconscious: as soon as I received something incredible and exciting, I would lose it.

Once I had figured out this story, I could see how it had played out in my life many times. And just to make this story a little more entertaining, I was in a doodling meditation one day and ended up drawing out a rough version of the camera that I had lost in the ivy when I was three. A few weeks before, I had asked my parents if they remembered me losing that camera. I asked because I wanted to know if anything else had happened around the situation, like me getting into trouble, and they had no clue what I was talking about.

After I created the doodle of the camera, I texted it to my parents, and my Dad was in disbelief! He said it was HIS favorite camera and thought that HE had lost it. He felt his Minolta SR-T 100 camera went missing during a move. I looked up the brand and model, and sure enough, that was the camera I remembered. So, it had never been my camera to begin with. It goes to show how many things we make up about ourselves. Sorry Dad, looks like I owe you one!

Regardless of whose camera it was, the story that I had created about myself, and the trends that kept playing out in my life because of it only confirmed that "I lost things whenever I got them." I shed light on a "rule" created from a simple story and can now bless the story in its entirety so that I no longer have to deal with this ever again. This recognition and acknowledgment is a method of self-coaching that will get you closer to a state of aligned and synchronistic flow.

I encourage you to do this work. It may take twenty to thirty minutes of sitting and allowing answers to come to you, or even longer. Once you clear these stories and trends, acknowledging them, things will start to shift.

Day Two: Individual Pattern Reflection & Discovery

More journaling ahead! Let's contemplate on all your past accomplished goals. What was your mindset at the time? Where did you feel less stressed and happier? What was your attitude, and what was your environment at the time?

Almost every time I'm talking to clients about their past goals and asking them these questions, they tell me they thought nothing of it at the time; it was a breeze to accomplish their goals. That's because when we are aligned with our goals and on the same wavelength as them, they come to us with increased speed.

What were your patterns, and how can you change the context and environment of your current life to support you getting back to that original psyche?

By gaining an understanding of your challenges, individuality, makeup, and becoming aware of the systems and processes that work for you, you can consciously implement them. There is no one size fits all solution!

For example, one of my coaching clients, a creative type, was having a lull point in his life and was not finding much work. He hired me, and we figured out his "Success Strategy". We analyzed his past successes and everything around those successes, from the people to his mindset, and here's what we came up with:

1- Belief- Someone else believed in him, and this created the introduction to an opportunity.

2- Connection- He felt wholly connected to the project and felt it happening with him.

3- Knowledge- His attitude had been 'Yes, of course, they'll hire me, the job is mine, I'm the only one for the position.'

4- Ownership of the project- He felt ownership, yet wasn't attached to the project. Next thing you know, clients would call and hire him.

Sometimes other people's methods for accomplishing goals can be challenging to apply to our life because everyone has a different process. Our goal is to find out what works best for you, what resonates where you can attain your goal and honor your individuality at the same time.

Make a list of your successes, manifestations, and wins from the past. Then consciously go through each item thinking about where you were at, mentally and in all other aspects, when you accomplished them. It could be anything: losing weight, meeting the love of your life, a job promotion, wins from your childhood like winning an enormous teddy bear at the grocery store.

What was happening internally and emotionally?

What was happening around you?

Did you feel in control?

Were you nonchalant about it?

Go through at least five successes that you come up with and see what trends you can create to find your personal "Success Strategy". If needed, talk to a friend about the goal, because sometimes verbalizing it helps you get a broader perspective. A breakdown and analysis process supports most everyone. The goal is to come up with three to five steps that you can understand and replicate when looking to create future aligned results.

You can then use this process for your current goals so that you can align them to your new Success Strategy. For my client, he needed to start with an introduction to the opportunity, based on a referral. He was to secure this as his first step, figuring out his most valuable players who would then support him and bring him leads and opportunities. He could then play out the rest of the steps to create aligned results.

Day Three: Are You Clear & Available?

Did the opportunity arise, and you weren't open or said 'No'? It's incredible how many times it happens, and we have absolutely no clue of it. When people write down goals, they often write about the outcome; here's a slightly skewed initial example from a client:

I want to make $150,000, and I want a house in the Hollywood Hills, I want a hot wife, two kids, and two dogs, I want to be an executive producer.

These goals are vague. Lots of space left for the imagination to fill in the blanks. When you go to a restaurant, you don't order a hamburger until you've read the description of the burger, and even then, when you place your order, you might still add or substitute things.

When you decide to go to Hawaii for vacation, you don't just buy a flight to Hawaii until you do some research on which island and what activities you want to participate in so that you can figure out precisely what island you'll be flying into and more.

The goals previously mentioned don't even state how often you'd be making $150,000. Is it in a week? A month? A year? What type of house is it, contemporary or classical? And this hot wife you want? Is she dramatic or sweet? What does 'hot' even mean? Possible additional thoughts on the kids and the dogs? And what does Executive Producer mean? Is it for commercials or movies?

The client needed much further defining, and here's why. I firmly believe that if you declare you will make $150,000 as part of your New Year's resolutions, you will have the opportunity to make that money. The question is: Are you open to receiving the payments? Are you willing to do what it takes?

Maybe job opportunities did come your way, but you said 'no' because they didn't feel right, although they may have paid you what you wanted to make that year. It didn't seem to be a fit, so you didn't take the job. However, the point is to notice that the opportunity did come your way! God did answer your New Year's resolution. Unfortunately, you weren't clear enough on exactly how you wanted it to manifest.

Have you heard of writing checks to yourself? Jim Carey shared that he had written a check to himself, ten years into the future, for $10,000,000 for acting services. Ten years later, he manifested exactly a ten million dollars role! I took this to heart and decided to write a check to myself for $15,000, due at the end of June, about four years ago. The funds had to do with the sales of my artwork.

Completely forgetting about my check to myself, I had an art show right before the end of June, at a friend's new house. He was also one of my real estate clients. He loved my work, and at the time, I'd custom create an art piece for all my real estate buyers. We decided to combine an open house and art show for extra entertainment.

All the art exhibited added to about $30,000. I didn't have many thoughts about how many I'd sell at the time. Diplaying my work and having a good time was more exciting to me. Later in the evening, a man came up to me and asked if he could buy all the work for his company for $15,000! Unfortunately, I was not ready to receive it yet. Instead, I stood in shock and disbelief. Having all my artwork sold in a flash second, along with the price point, put me in a state of shock. Combine the offer with my attachment to the paintings, and you'll see pure resistance to being provided for by the Universe! Within less then a second and with no thought, I blurted out 'NO!'. I'm even laughing at myself as I write this. I didn't battle with negotiating a different price. I shrieked 'NO' with my heart rate somewhat elevated.

Two days later, I realized what I had done. I reached out to the man to attempt negotiations and never heard back. Who knows, maybe he wasn't as serious as he seemed. Regardless, I later realized how I'd manifested what I "wanted": a $15,000 offer for my artwork and within three days of June 30th. Sadly, I hadn't been clear in my check writing about how many sold art pieces equaled the $15,000, nor had I done the mental work needed to detach myself from the art pieces to let them go. I had actualized an offer but wasn't open to receiving it at these specific enough terms.

In these instances where you are aware of what happened, it's important to say 'thank you' for the opportunity and be grateful that your wishes came true. Then go back to your dream drawing board and get clear on exactly what you're looking to achieve.

Also, there are times when you do not need to feel bad about saying 'NO'; trust your body! I received this question from someone who's looking to be an actor. She already had school, work, and a trip planned for July when an acting opportunity came along. She was excited to have the opportunity, yet it was a low paying gig, and it would have cost her money with lost work and changing flights to accept the job. She was nervous that if she said 'No' to the gig (and the Universe), she wouldn't get another one. I recommended she be grateful that an opportunity came her way and to use it as a way of gaining clarity, to let the Heavens know more clearly what type of jobs she was looking for. This way, she would be fully open to receiving when the dream job came her way!

Day Four: Create Your Virtual Reality

I would love to have the technology to start a virtual reality company where you could create your dreams and then live them daily! Just put on those VR "dream" goggles for twenty to thirty minutes and check out your envisioned reality. If this is something you're able to create, definitely get in touch. Some people are paralyzed and told they could never walk again. They put on the VR goggles and step into a walking program for about an hour to two a day, which allows them to build the neural synapses needed so they can walk[6]; they understand that walking is a possibility for them. And it becomes a reality! They train their brains to walk again! How powerful is this?

In the meantime, we'll have to do with the tech available to us. The goal of this chapter is to create that virtual reality experience with your Best Day Ever and your aligned dreams. If needed, check back through each line to make sure it's in alignment with your body. The point is to always be in alignment with everything you do. The more you practice listening to your body about what you are creating, the more immediate and innate this process will become for you. The ultimate goal is to be in flow and in alignment every moment, always aware of the messages your body is sending you.

Now that you have your Best Day Ever dialed let's figure out what type of learning is most natural for you.

Are you auditory or visual?

---

[6] https://www.forbes.com/sites/delltechnologies/2018/01/16/how-vr-is-helping-paraplegics-walk-again/#4b30613875d0

How do you like to get through books, by reading or by listening?

Do you need to read them out loud, or to another person?

Do you need to physically be part of the process?

Does the process need to be shared because you are a social learner?

Some people need to be in complete isolation in order to learn. We want to discover what type of learning suits you best.

If you are an auditory learner, like I am, I encourage you to get your phone and record the reading of your Best Day with lots of love, compassion, and excitement. Then, every morning and night, take a moment to listen to it as a way to start your day on the right foot and end your day with clarity, as you drift off to sleep.

If you're a visual learner, create a dream or vision board with many images related to what a day in your best life would include. I've had clients in the entertainment industry edit vision movies, instead of vision boards that they can watch daily. You can also read what you wrote every day, possibly out loud. I challenge you to do this for thirty days in a row! Also, when you go to sleep with this kind of vision, your mind will be working on it while you're sleeping and you could awake with new ideas supporting your mission!

The kinesthetic learner needs to step into the dream. If your goal has to do with a home that's not yet yours, start going to open houses and experience yourself walking through them as if they were your own. Imagine you just got home and were walking to the kitchen to make a delicious meal. Mark that experience in your memory to tap into the feelings regularly, let your body absorb it. Test drive the car you're after.

When an advertising client was pitching a campaign for a product, she'd often go to the store where the product was sold and pretended she was shopping for it. Also, she would walk about the product aisle, secretly watching those who came towards the product to see how they were around it. She'd look at how they experienced their options, and then stopped to ask them questions. Another good example of this is the movie *What Women Want*, with Mel Gibson, where his character decides to experience all the feminine products to tap into the female mind. These are examples of what I'm encouraging you to do; it can be easy and fun since you're doing it for yourself!

As a social learner, read this vision to your friends, so they are clear on it; by sharing it, they will hold this vision for you, and you will have read it out loud, which is also powerful. If you are more of a silent manifester, go into a twenty-minute meditation, close your eyes and step into your Best Day Ever.

Fully immerse yourself into this day, experience all the feelings, all the sensations, radiate a big smile as you go through it, and don't hesitate to open your arms wide into a Y (Yes) stance of receiving as well. Imagine it is all real and available to you in the NOW.

What do you feel? Giddiness? Excitement? Gratitude? Pure delight or confidence? Feel it and become it!

Make this part of your Miracle Morning (a concept from the book by Hal Elrod), or, as I call it, the Magic Hour. Try it out for thirty days, if you are reading this with your accountability group- message so you can mark as complete each day for thirty days. I call it a thirty-days of magic; figure out your best practice and do it for thirty days in a row, consistently.

You can also add your 'I AM' affirmations to the Best Day Ever process. State your 'I AM's clearly. Pick one each day to say over and over throughout the day. I know people who set a two-hour timer on their phone to remind them to stop whatever they are doing and check back into their vision. I love this idea; however, I often find myself in meetings when the alarm goes off, so it wouldn't work for me. Figure out what's most actionable for you. In the event you decide to change up your vision, start your thirty-day process over again. I usually do a new one at the start of every month.

Day Five: Receive- Say Yes

Do you have any issues receiving? Opportunities are coming your way every single day. It could be that the next-door neighbor offered to pick up something at the grocery store for you, and you said 'No, thanks' because you didn't want to be a burden... although you needed some milk. Or maybe a friend offered to buy both of you coffees during your coffee date, yet you didn't want them to as you were planning on paying for both as well, instead, you said 'No, thank you.'

The goal is to start noticing how many times you say 'No' throughout the day and to the most mundane things! As soon as I did this exercise, I remembered a friend had offered to take out my trash, and I had said no because it was my trash, and they didn't need to deal with my trash! Other examples popped up: someone offering to drive me home instead of me taking an Uber, and me saying no because I didn't want to be a nuisance to them even though they offered. Ridiculous, the excuses we make to keep us from receiving.

What would it take for you to live a 'Yes' life? You deserve to receive it! The faster you start accepting the smallest gifts, the sooner you start receiving the large ones too. You now will be telling the Universe 'Yes, I accept, thank you.'

It could be as simple as someone offering you water when you go to their house or a piece of pizza when you are dairy and gluten-free. What about accepting it for now, and maybe having just one bite? Of course, not if your health is at risk. Think of the last time you were around someone who said 'No, I don't do that' or 'No, I don't need help'... how did it make you feel as you were offering to help?

I challenged a client to this once, and she came back to me sharing that she was saying 'No' four or five times a day. Even to this day, when someone offers her help, she often says

'No, thanks, I got it,' yet inside she's struggling and could use the help, with three kids and a husband who often travels.

The shift is realizing that we are worthy of receiving support. It starts with the simple act of saying "Yes, that would be awesome!". And remember, the 'Yes' mode is expansive while the 'No' mode is constrictive.

Days Six - Seven: Signs

We're going to open you up even more today. It's time to receive even more. You'll be learning about the guidance of signs.

When fully grounded in vision and what one is creating, signs have magical power. As signs come in, you want to use them. Learn about paying attention, being in gratitude for the guidance, or looking in the mirror if the direction isn't coming through. You may be having trouble connecting.

I first started paying attention to signs when three of my friends committed suicide within a month. It was awful. Talk about a wake-up call to awareness!

I had recently moved to LA, and a friend from Portland, Brent, let me know that he would be in town in a few weeks and wanted to meet up. I said 'Yes.' I wasn't super close to him, but we had shared some moments around startups and entrepreneurship ventures, and I always found him to be very authentic and open in his communication.

Brent passed on about two weeks after he had contacted me. The day he left this Earth, I thought to myself that I should reach out and see when he would be arriving. That night, I woke up very early, having had a dream about him and decided I would reach out later that day to share the funniness of it while also checking in as to when he'd be in town. Sadly, when I hopped on Facebook that morning, the news of his death was everywhere. I had no idea he was in a dark place. Then I thought 'What if I had reached out yesterday. when I first thought of reaching out? Maybe my reaching out would have reminded him of his fun upcoming trip to LA?'. I know this wasn't my responsibility, yet the synchronicity left me perplexed.

During the same month, my friend Kris reached out; he was someone I talked to once a year. He had been good friends with my ex-husband, so it was usually somewhat of a detached conversation at a party or event. Every time we spoke, it was generally about referring business to each other, although I had always felt a deep connection to him. He was an extremely compassionate individual, and his family was his life.

When he randomly reached out, I was surprised by his call. He wanted to know how my new life in Los Angeles was and how my first book, *Man-Erisms*, was coming along. Kris had also just moved to a new state and seemed to be settling in with the family and making new friends.

This time we had about a ten-fifteen minute phone call, and after hanging up, I realized this call had nothing to do with business at all. I thought to myself that it was odd that he had called. These questions popped up in my mind, but they were not substantial enough for me to dig deeper. I brushed it off as him being an amazing person who checked in on the people he cared about. Disturbingly enough, within a couple of weeks, the news broke out that he had taken his own life. I sent him and his family love and light.

Lastly, Alan was more of an acquaintance. We had met multiple times because we had a friend in common, Justin, who used to be one of my roommates. These experiences were my first real awareness of signs. Justin kept popping up in my mind for no clear reason, I kept releasing the thoughts. I hadn't talked to him in over a year after my move to California. What got me to call him, beyond the random thoughts of him, was that one day, I was waiting in line and the person at the service counter kept calling out the name Justin, who was nowhere to be seen, so she kept yelling the name. I knew I needed to call him, so as soon as I left, I did.

Justin was surprised by my call. We had a casual talk, he kept saying that life was good and then turning it around to ask me how LA was. Although we hadn't spoken in a long time, I knew Justin since fifth grade and could be very honest and direct with him. Eventually, I told him that I kept receiving signs for the past couple weeks and that there had to be something more for my call, asking him flat out what was he not sharing.

I wonder if he thought I was crazy. He opened up, sharing that his friend Alan had committed suicide a week and a half before. I had had no idea of this unfortunate story. Alan's downward spiral resulting in suicide had baffled many.

At this point, Justin had been popping up in my mind for two weeks. This suicide was also the third one in a month, confirming my sensitivity and connectedness to others. These three deaths became my breaking point into awareness of signs. I acknowledged them knowing they were everywhere.

From that moment on, anytime I have a random thought about someone, I reach out at once. Signs are here for a reason, and I could no longer let them pass by. I knew I had the tools to dig in with curiosity and ask questions during meditation, as well.

Often, there are many things going on in our lives that we don't notice these random thoughts that pop up, so we brush them off as if they never happened.

Wouldn't you want to pick up on these signs and possible warnings?

I also learned that many signs show up in threes, so when they do- jump! I have story after story of this, now that the signs have become clear as day to me. Part of the reason I get consistent signs is that I am continuously grateful for them.

A couple of weeks ago, I opened up my email to find this weirdly written message about a speaking opportunity in London. I say it was weird because of the way text comes through when someone writes to me directly through my website: there are no paragraphs, it's just one huge blob. Also, the English used seemed a little off. So I thought it was a spam message and dismissed the email.

Within 24 hours, a few things happened that I would never have previously given much thought to, and because they all arrived within a short period, I decided to give it some clout. First, my friend decided she was going to throw a party at her place because her sister had just moved back from London. Then I was talking to a few girlfriends who decided they wanted to go on a London girls' getaway. The next day, another girlfriend and I were at a restaurant where four Brits approached us. These synchronistic scenarios were just the beginning. The entire week London was popping up everywhere. That week a cousin that I don't speak to except for at large family gatherings had a baby and guess where they live... in London.

I had been requesting manifestation in opportunities for speaking at events in other countries. And here was a possibility that was precisely what I wanted, yet it came in a form that I was unfamiliar with, so I had rejected it! Luckily, the signs were adding up so much that I became aware of them and remembered the email; I responded, asking for more information. While I am writing this, we're in negotiations for the event.

A soul sister of mine, phenomenal author Gabby Bernstein, also often talks about signs. At the launch of her book, *Super Attractor*, she shared about how she likes to request specific signs. Some people ask for butterflies, in this instance Gabby requested the cardinal bird. Within a few days she was on the phone with a friend in their car. During their conversation, the friend shared a cardinal landed on her windshield. The friend didn't have a clue about Gabby's previous sign request. So now, she had her answer. The cardinal supported her knowing her decision was aligned and on the right track.

The Universe is always responding to our requests. When you think about what you want or what you don't want, you are gifted just that. Ask, and you shall receive! Remember, the answers to your requests may not come in the form that you thought they would, that is why it's so important to take those extra moments to become extremely clear, concise, and intentional in everything you do.

As you become more and more present, the signs will stand out because you are aware of them.

Has this ever happened to you: you decide you are going to buy a car, let's say a vintage late 60's E-Type Jaguar convertible with a gorgeous wooden steering wheel, thinking that it's unique and you'd be one of the few to own this car. You absolutely love it and can't wait to have it. As you drive around, you start noticing that every other car is a vintage Jag. When did that happen? You see, they are everywhere and now can be easily attainable.

Similarly, let's say you're dying to have that vintage 60s E-Type convertible, and you're frustrated that you don't have the money to buy it. You keep receiving signs that you don't have the money to buy the vintage car of your dreams. You start noticing them everywhere, confirming that you don't have the vehicle or the money to buy it.

Do you see the difference? Increasing your frequencies shifts your perspective; positivity is paramount in getting what you want. One thought is light, and the other one is heavy. Signs are here to support you. Should you feel that they are coming to you in a negative light, pay attention, and see what you can shift. How does your mindset have you held hostage? Could it use some love and light to change the point from which you perceive? The last thing you want is to lose an opportunity.

If you feel that you aren't getting any signs, put it into your intentions and prayer requests. Ask for support in receiving signs, maybe even make a specific symbol a sign for you. Some people have numbers such as 11's that show up during specific situations. One of my numbers is 11, hence the book launch on 11/11. I might see it as 11:11, 11, $1.11, and to me, this combination of numbers can mean 'be aware,' 'watch out,' 'just notice', new beginnings, etc. When I see a significant amount, I pause and notice what I was thinking about, what actions I was doing, and who I was with, to see if there is some other guidance there for me. My Dad has me saved in his phone as Bethany and my number. He likes to call me when he sees the specific time as a number because he thinks it's so funny.

Other people might ask for a butterfly or an owl, as a sign. You can get as broad or specific as you'd like. You could also be open to a symbol that is gifted to you. I didn't ask for 911 to be my number. Regardless, don't hesitate to ask for support, and you will be provided for.

The biggest takeaway is to note when things happen in threes, symbols developing your awareness. Maybe you ask your questions in the morning and don't receive a response, yet you end up with three signs throughout the next couple of days that give you the answer you were craving. When something pops up three times, and you have no idea why, sit down and feel into with your questions or meditations for further exploration.

Dear Spirit of the Highest Truth and Light,
I'm noticing this _____ happening and am seeking to find the purpose of it benefiting my life in the highest and best way. Is there something I should be extra aware of?

If you still have trouble receiving signs or tapping into awareness, look into removing the walls that are blocking your perception of the signs, which you may have built up throughout life. Also, understand that not receiving a sign is a sign in itself. Start with asking your inner child about the difficulties of having awareness.

Dear 3-year-old Bethany,
I'm having trouble receiving guidance and signs, do you have any thoughts on something that may be keeping my awareness of signs at bay?

Try drawing or doodling on it to see what happens. You are your own biggest block and can also be your most prominent advocate. I'm removing blocks all the time. Don't be discouraged. The awareness will lead you to where you need to go!

SUMMARY - LEAVES & SEEDS

Day 1: Our Individual Patterns - Past Goals
• List out the goals you have yet to carry out.
• Meditate on the stories and trends that have been recurring in your life. Do some extra digging for added clarity.

Day 2: Individual Pattern Reflection & Discovery
• Look at past results and come up with a three to five step Success Strategy, understanding what has happened in the past that lead to success, so that you can replicate it moving forward.

Day 3: Are You Clear and Available?
• Take a moment to look at your goals and your Best Day Ever. Are you specific enough, or are there a lot of open-ended possibilities?
• Can you think of any opportunities that came your way where you said 'No', because they didn't seem right? It's important to note these wins, even though you didn't accept them.

Day 4: Create Your Virtual Reality
• Figure out your best learning style.
• Experience your Best Day Ever so you can build new neural synapses. Make it a 30-day practice!

Day 5: Receive - Say 'Yes'

• Start saying 'Yes' to the smallest things: someone holding the door open for you, or offering you a glass of water. Notice all the times you say 'No' throughout the day. Would the outcome have been different, had you answered 'Yes'?

Days 6 & 7: Signs

• Start asking questions to your chosen Mentor and be open to receive guidance and answers.

Which seed that you've planted this week gave your body the biggest jolt of excitement?

WEEK SEVEN – SUN
VIBRATE AT A NEW INTENSITY

Trees would not survive without light, and neither would you. Even sunlight can power a house, via solar panels. Light is an energy force that supports your knowing that you are aligned and in your truth. Remember, truth is light. When you feel light, life feels blissful as though you are vibrating at increased wavelengths. To add to this, I want you to be tingling from head to toe. Tingling is the ultimate experience of being in truth and knowing the power of your body intelligence as a path to achieve aligned results. Seriously, who couldn't use some more sun in their life?

This week we're going to bring your levels up a notch by adding some sparkle into your life. We raise our vibrations and broadcasting energy to tap into the most beneficial guidance. You have advanced over the past weeks to a higher energetic frequency level. You may not believe it, yet look over what's happened in the past few weeks as you've read this book; even the smallest positive shifts create a ripple effect.

The higher our vibration level, the easier it is to reach the guidance within. Being aligned to the goals supports us in attracting everything that we choose. Each intention and goal holds a vibration level. There is a vibrational number associated with everything; you can feel it, based merely on how you feel throughout the day. For example, your mornings could either have a higher or lower frequency level, depending on whether you are a morning or evening person.

How great it would be if we were all at higher energy levels! As you work through this book, your energy levels lift so you can level up as well. In preparation for opening up the self to body intelligence and alignment, you will learn specific ways to increase your energy levels.

Day One: Overwhelm Yourself in Gratitude

Today is about being grateful. For the good, the bad, and the ugly! As you start entering into a practice of gratitude, your perspectives will also naturally begin to change.

Did you ever participate in the "100 days of Happiness Challenge" on the social media platforms? The challenge consisted in taking a picture every day of something that made you feel happy and posting it on Instagram or Facebook. I finished this challenge, and it brought me so much happiness, because I was searching for it constantly! Every day, I was on the hunt for joy! It was pretty phenomenal, even on days that were less than joyous, when I may have felt like that was the last thing

I wanted to do. Still, I'd find a particular moment that did bring some light into my life, because I was determined to do 100 days in a row. Just the fact that I figured out what that moment was going to be lifted my spirits.

Similarly, we are going to get into a state of being grateful ALL DAY LONG. Take on the #100daysofblessings on Facebook, Instagram, or blog about it. There's always a way to consider yourself blessed. For everything in your life: friends, family, your chosen family, clothes, food, a green light, the bills that you are paying... Start saying the mantras:

"I am so blessed because _____"

"I am so grateful and thankful for _____"

I am so grateful and thankful for the time on the phone with my Mom today. I am so grateful and thankful for this delicious watermelon iced tea that I'm drinking. I am so grateful and thankful for this speeding ticket that I just got because it teaches me to slow down so I can enjoy each moment and stay safe (commenting from a place of responsibility).

Try incorporating this message from the moment you wake up until you go to sleep — no reason to wait until the end of the day to count your blessings.

And should you want to start up the photo challenge again, go for it with #100daysofblessings! Post about the moments you are grateful for every day, and keep yourself accountable by dating them Day 1, etc. Do not worry about what others think, it's all part of your breakthroughs! This is for YOU.

Day Two: Sparkle in Abundance

Let's take our practice to another level: this day's exercise is about wealth and abundance, capitalizing on being present and aware of everything that we are feeling and experiencing, within and externally. Don't be afraid of money; you deserve wealth! Use the steps described in the previous weeks, if you felt any discomfort when you read the above statements, to conquer any blocks around money.

Many situations in life are caught up in "the lack of" or "not good enough" mindset. Think about childhood games, for example, like Red Rover, Heads Up Seven Up, and Musical Chairs. Children are taught from a young age that they need to stand out, or they may not get noticed with Heads Up Seven Up. In Red Rover, they learn that they not only need to be better so that they are selected, they also need to break through others to get ahead. They are taught that there isn't enough for everyone, with the Musical Chairs and they must be better than others if they want to get ahead. This gets ingrained in our subconscious and bodies from an early age. There's no reason to be better than others, or get ahead of them, when you acknowledge all that is here for you and know your truth in abundance.

First, let's capitalize on the air around you. There is never a lack of oxygen for your body to inhale and keep going throughout the day. How powerful is that? You are surrounded by abundant air allowing you to function. You can have conversations with those you love. You can eat the plentiful food available to you.

How about your friends and family, which may also be your chosen family? Acknowledge the abundance in them and in what the connection with them offers your mind, body and soul. Connected conversations are rich with emotional energy that can fuel you.

It's also time to acknowledge your skills and personality traits. In my first short book, *Man-Erisms*, I suggested people take a moment to write down all their abilities. Even if you don't consider yourself exceptional at something, the simple fact that you can do it is great. Let's think of a guitar player. To me, knowing that you can play the guitar is incredible, whether you are a paid musician or not. What traits would your friends and family say you have? Maybe you are excellent at defusing arguments. That's special! Acknowledge the abundance of beautiful qualities that you have; yes, you can fill a whole notebook. It may be difficult at first, but you do have an abundance of qualities.

Let's move on to financial abundance, to make you aware of the wealth around you. As you read this book, how much did it cost you? Are you reading it on an iPad or a tablet? How much did that cost you? How much did the chair that you are sitting in cost? Are you listening to the book in your car? Even if you don't own or pay for it, you are experiencing prosperity.

When you're in a car, a Lyft, or bus, they most likely cost quite a bit. Start looking at everything you are using in your life as $$$ signs. The frequency of wealth and abundance surrounds you! That's what money is; it's an energy and frequency exchange.

As I'm writing this, I can apply the same rule to my once $2000+ computer, sitting on a $100,000,000 airplane, with a $400 plane ticket, my $800 phone, $100/month cell phone service, and $900 iPad while traveling to see my best friend as she's about to give birth. Just think of the $$$ spent on all the equipment, hospital, and staff for a delivery! I'm surrounded by so much wealth and abundance at all times, and so are you.

Even when you don't feel like you have any money, look at every little thing around you so that you can experience the wealth surrounding you. As you go about your day, pay attention, be aware of these little nuggets of gold.

This may seem like mere money talk; the practice is about being present and aware. It is meant to shed a different light on your life and shift you into a new perspective about things.

If you're feeling queasy, listen to your body. Some people are astonishingly uncomfortable with money. Now is your time to figure out the reasons you think this way so that you can acknowledge it and open yourself up to receive. It could be the reason why you haven't been offered a raise at your job or a particular opportunity you've been longing for. A chance to free yourself from self-imposed boundaries and open to the abundance that's all around is available.

Recently I went on a girls' trip for my sister's birthday in Playa del Carmen, Mexico. My sister wanted a tropical vacation where we didn't have to worry about anything, so she organized and planned the whole thing and selected an all-inclusive hotel. Well, this girl has never experienced an inclusive spot before, so within the first hour, it already felt life-changing.

The super friendly staff was consistently serving us as we jumped into the main pool. I'd be thinking about how they were trying to make their profits by continually bringing us drinks and food. Yet this was an all-inclusive resort. They wanted us to enjoy ourselves and have a great time together. It was so odd to select such delectables off the menu, not thinking about the cost. I told myself to cement this experience within me to know that I can recall it at any time. I didn't realize how conscious I was of what I was spending and how overbearing it was in my life.

Wouldn't it be great not to have the burden of money? When we start to shift into gratitude for what's around us, it supports lifting that weight off our shoulders. Yes, it may be easier said than done. That's why the experience of being at the hotel was so great for me. I love experiential workshops because it supports cementing an experience in my body so that it knows from there on out of fresh possibilities. Don't worry. You don't need to go and sign up for a workshop at this moment. However, if you set up an accountability group, they would be valuable here for holding each other responsible in acknowledging your gratitude and blessings.

You can also bring this experience into a meditation. Take a moment to close your eyes, experiencing the wealth that is all around. Know that you are fully taken care of. Close your eyes for a few minutes and as you drift out, ask yourself how this feels and looks. I use the word KNOWING because when you are in the state of knowing, you are unwavering. Your whole body is concrete with the knowledge of an experience. What starts happening to your body when you feel the prosperity all around? How about when you know that the Universe has your back and is working for you?

Be in the moment, with prosperity and wealth, so that you can fully realize fortune around you and your value in experiencing it all. Start having your days sparkle with the Universal Wealth that is always surrounding you. Tap into it, allowing the intelligence of your body to fully consume it and radiate it back out into the world.

Day Three: Paint the Town in Smiles

Smile. Practice smiling today! A smile lifts your energy levels instantly. Each time you smile, picture yourself elevating your intuitive skills and manifestation skills. Smile at yourself in the mirror, smile as you take a shower, smile at people as you walk down the street. Don't worry about feeling goofy (goofy is an excellent frequency level, by the way), rejection, or not getting a smile back. Just smile, it's for you, and when others receive your smile, they will also be lifted by about ten points. It is such a simple thing to do, a real miracle worker!

Today is the day to smile your heart out. Simple things can create such a magical impact. You may read this, huff and puff about it, or you may read it and already be smiling right now. Doesn't it feel good? Smiling is contagious.

While you work, exercise, walk, eat, keep those smiles flowing about abundantly. You have so much to be grateful for, so don't forget to continue tapping into the abundance of the world.

On a physical level, smiling helps your health by boosting your immune system. One study found that it supported white cell counts[7]. Smiling increases your dopamine and endorphin levels. When you smile, your body reacts and feels that everything is "right" in the world. This sensation then supports your body by lowering the fight or flight response and cortisol levels, which means you are reducing stress and dis-ease within yourself. If you're lowering cortisol levels, that means you could use smiling as something to support weight loss too. Smiling is so amazing!

I'm smiling as I write this, and in turn, I'm feeling my whole body - my Being - smile from the inside out. It's that powerful, and you're automatically projecting it out into the world. Let's get you to align with those higher energy levels,

---

[7] https://www.ncbi.nlm.nih.gov/pubmed/21983400

such as energies of love, so that you are closer in alignment with your goals.

Day Four: Grounding in Intention

This practice supports my mornings and weeks, starting on a high note, and it can support yours too. The exercise brings growth, ease, and wins - surprise blessings every day.

You can start this exercise any day. Myself, I start my week by grounding in intention, every Sunday evening. I like to make it a game, so I can check-in at the end of the week and see what I've accomplished. Sometimes my goals are reached that week, and sometimes I'll see them move on to the next week and the future. There's always an excuse not to do the exercise, so it is crucial that you ground yourself and take a moment and tune in to being a catalyst for change in your life. Get excited about the new life you are unleashing!

I first started with just Sunday evenings, and now my practice has moved on to every morning. On days when I wake up late or have an early morning appointment that I run off to, I'll take a moment at the end of the day to look back and notice that it has been a more hectic and chaotic day. Other times, I'll do my intention exercise while driving to my early appointment.

Although it may be difficult at first to take the time on Sunday evenings or every morning, once you create a pattern, it becomes habitual. Once you realize the difference between the days and the weeks when you ground in intention and those when you don't, you'll create the time to make it happen as the reward is greater than the effort.

The easiest way to create a habit is by planning the new activity around another one you are used to doing. For example, you could say "I love you" or "I'm grateful for ..." in the mirror every time you brush your teeth -which is hopefully a morning habit for you. My morning practice used to be that I'd wake up, make my amazing coffee concoction, and then head back to bed for journaling. Then I got a dog, so I now am working on figuring out new patterns.

Did you know that when new songs are released and are intended for top hits, radio networks are often paid to play the new songs between two existing top hits? The method creates a connection in your brain to support your loving the new songs, thus making them the next top hits. By adding intention, awareness, and meditation to something you already do, they will become a new habit, naturally.

It is also necessary to be specific when outlining your intentions. When you think to yourself "I am going to find the woman of my dreams", it sounds like a great affirmation and a purposeful, solid starting point. However, you must address the details and the reasons for your intention:

Why is this important to you?

What experiences will finding the woman of your dreams bring you?

What are the details of this dream woman?

Almost every intention could be detailed further. When we shoot from the hip without a clear target in mind, we might end up where we don't want to be.

Creating habits like grounding in intention, every morning, and every week, will up your level of alignment and manifest a brand new life for you.

Every thought you think is creating the world you live in. Every idea is an affirmation of intention. This is why it is crucial to clear the chaos so you can bring the real you and your beautiful soul to the forefront. Daily living by intention allows you to come back to what you've created that morning with a little bit more ease.

Another key helping factor for grounding in intention is connecting to your divine source. Connect to God, connect to your soul, connect to multiple sources, should you choose to.

When talking to my mother, a hard-core Catholic, we tend to get caught up on words: for example, 'intention' is to me what 'prayer' is to her. My mother likes to go to church every single morning. I used to judge her, but now I see it as my mom's time to meditate. I am not that much different, as I too take time every morning to meditate on my goals and the ways I can support others. I don't call it 'prayer', yet that's basically what it is!

The definition of prayer: a solemn request for help or an expression of thanks addressed to God or an object of worship. An earnest hope or wish.

With the definition of prayer in mind, you can see why it is perfect for your morning's Magic Hour: conceiving how to set up your day, and expressing all that you're grateful for.

When you are writing or thinking of your morning or Sunday evening intentions, first, take a moment and connect to God or Love. When you feel a shift in your being towards lightness or tingles, you are connected.

After connecting, you can clarify your intentions. You can find my meditation for this process online. Next, release your requests into the Universe, with a lightness about it. Bring in the experience of achieving your goals. Feel the gratitude for achieving results.

Give extra attention to the connection before sending out your requests. Here's an example that shows why: I went to my friend's company gathering at a local bowling alley. The first round was playful. I tried different balls with different weights and finger holes. Each time I rolled the ball, my goal and intention were to get a strike, of course. That didn't happen. When it came to the second game, I decided to connect first, then bring intention to every single roll. I got up to the lane and stood there for a moment with the bowling ball. I connected to God first, feeling the lightness and tingles, then I visualized myself throwing the ball and it going right down the center of the lane and creating a perfect strike. Then, I released that ball. This game was the best scoring I have ever had in my life. For eight of the ten turns, I either had a strike or a spare. Everyone thought I was a pro bowler who had bluffed the first game!

During the last game, I felt I was taking up too much time with my process of intention as I visualized every throw, so I lightened it up. Instead, I just witnessed in my mind's eye the ball going straight down the lane for a strike. Then I threw it. It was intentional and visual, yet without the connection process. Ultimate fail! Granted, this was still a higher scoring game than the first one, which was a pure intention that revolved around pure fun. Adding the foundational connection process ultimately was a huge difference. Taking the extra moment to connect to God first and then to visualize my intention with the throw was amazing. The connection was the missing piece.

There are similar examples of athletes and performers: before they go on stage or the field. They often huddle with their teams and pray. Even if they don't believe in a God, they still pray. Visualizing the goal, they ask for support from a force greater than themselves.

Tap into the connection with God or the Universe. Feel that light tingle before making requests, asking questions, or creating your Best Day Ever. The connection piece supports you in aligning to your truth, body, of course, those goals you're crushing now with ease.

Days Five through Seven: Extra Support

In the event you're experiencing a rut or what may feel like a downward spiral, there are ways to work through them, and we're going to address them. Remember that trees can consume the water from a flash flood, and with healthy practices of body intelligence, you can also use unpredictable situations to your advantage.

Trauma happens and can fire you up in significant ways bringing you down into the trenches with one swift piece of news, sometimes even numbing your mind, body, and soul so that they feel absolutely nothing. I'd love to get you out of it with this book, yet don't hesitate to call for support.

Let's get outside and get some sunshine. Getting sunlight supports regulating your production of melatonin as well, according to Dr. Breus, the Sleep Doctor[8]. A good snooze also will help your mood. Also, taking a walk outdoors will support aligning your body physically and energetically. Even if you don't feel like it, walk tall so that you are putting your body into a state of expansion; your body does the work of shifting energy levels for you.

Try an animal sanctuary where you can be with the animals focusing all attention on them. When feeling stuck, shifting your focus from yourself to someone else, being kind, or supporting a cause that you feel strongly about, can open you to another awareness level.

---

8 https://thesleepdoctor.com/how-to-sleep-better

Take a trip, try the mountains or beaches. Find yourself in awe of the extraordinary real-life paintings in front of you, the mountain, or ocean. Sit with feet grounded in the earth or sand. Do your best to connect with the planet and your truth. Relax, free from distraction, as you acknowledge your connection to the world. I love to go snowboarding by myself and be one with nature. More often, though, you'll find me walking to the beach and sitting in meditation while taking in the massive ocean. One of my favorite things is floating in the water. As I drift up and down with the rolling waves, I am at complete surrender to the water holding me, knowing it's got my back. I think it's one of the most peaceful things I do in life, at least when there aren't a ton of people around.

When you are in nature, possibly hiking, you are hopefully walking amongst luscious green plants. When you are around living plants, you know that they are in the vibrational energy of alignment. Naturally, being amongst them, you are breathing in their aligned energy. It's so beautiful.

Then, of course, trees help us tap into the earth with ease. Never hesitate when walking by them to place a hand out and touch them. Feel free to be a tree hugger as well. Trees are connected to the earth and to each other. They can bring you the love and support you need.

I had heard of this concept of connecting with the trees before yet took it with a grain of salt. I liked the thought of it though, as I love my hikes, snowboarding, and mountain biking amongst the trees. There's a particular spot in Marina del Rey,

CA that I like to go that's full of trees and also looking at the jetty going out to the ocean. One day, as I was sitting on a bench amongst the trees, with a marina view, I felt my body called to a tree. I went over and touched it. I stood for a moment and then experienced a further motion to get closer. I leaned up against the tree, and it still wasn't feeling right. I felt the tree energy magnetically encourage me to sit on it, climb a bit, and sit on its trunk. I was feeling a little awkward, yet I love to follow the guidance, so I followed suit. Within seconds of sitting, unexpected tears were streaming down my face. I was shocked, yet instantly comforted in ways I didn't know I needed.

Although it might sound silly, I encourage you to sit with your back up to a tree. Tune into your heart. Experience the heart opening to be a receptor of the tree's energy. Allow yourself to receive the support, love, and wisdom of this tree. Let it be a connection point with the earth below that holds you up every day and the light energy that beams from the sun to the leaves. Breathe in the fresh oxygen provided by the tree. Allow the oxygenated air to carry out all the negativity in your body, mind, and soul so that you may become one with the planet and the Universe. Just be.

Furthermore, in Feng Shui, we are advised to place our furniture in the spot the dog lies, for good luck. Where the dog lies is a happy spot. My last dog, Kessler, would always lay down at the base of the biggest tree around anytime we were hanging outside. The trees were most definitely his place of joy. Find yourself a big beautiful tree to enjoy.

SUMMARY - SUN

Day One: Overwhelm Yourself in Gratitude
- "I am so grateful and thankful for _____"
- Throughout the day, say this phrase in your head, and whenever you have the chance, say it out loud.

Day 2: Sparkle in Abundance
- Pay attention to all types of abundance around you.
- How do they add value to your life?
- Let your being absorb this Universal Wealth.

Day 3: Paint the Town in Smiles
- Smile your heart out with love to you and everyone you meet, allow that beautiful smile to lift your spirits.

Day 4: Grounding in Intention
- Set your intentions for the day and week.
- Experience the subtle shifts throughout the day, compared to previously.

Days 5 through 7: Extra Support
- Get outside, experience the vast and wondrous beauty available to you.
- Find a tree to connect too.

Have you experienced any tingling sensations that you can hold on to?

AFTER NOW

Now that you have fully connected to your body, truth, earth, hopefully, an extraordinary tree, the Universe, and the present, what's next? You want to keep the guidance and information flowing. Which it always is; however, things can come and pop up in our lives instantly throwing us off-balance.

Keep the book close by for support when in need of recalibration of your alignment and body intelligence. Don't hesitate to close your eyes, ask for divine wisdom, then open the book up to a random page. Know you were guided to precisely what will serve you best and forward at that moment.

Staying in tune with your body intelligence is critical for moving forward with people and relationships, as well. As you become the ultimate user of your body intelligence, you will also become extremely aware when at meetings, events, talking with school teachers, the server at a restaurant, the customer service person on the other end of the phone line, and your employees as well. Your emotional intelligence will also grow when connecting with others. Your body will tell you via expansion, lightness, heaviness, or constriction, where you need to go with the other person.

Feel each experience when communicating with people, and when you look at them in the eyes.

What do you see, hear, and smell with your body?

Does your body trust them?

Does your body tell you that maybe they are having a bad day or aren't well for some reason?

What is your body sharing in each moment with every decision that you make? Time for consciousness. Continue to experience life in new ways; trusting your body will lead the way.

One of my business managers was among the people who have read the first draft of this book. He shared that when he went into a very lucrative meeting which promised him the world, it didn't feel right. He felt his stomach twisting during the conversation. Although his mind didn't want to, he turned down their million-dollar offer. His mind was fighting him the whole way, yet he was surrendering to his body and truth, using the guidance of this book. Within a week, a company he had previously worked with made him an even stronger offer for something different, and he graciously accepted. He felt and knew in his body that it was the right decision. He realized how listening to his body had supported him. Had he taken the previous offer, he wouldn't have been able to work with the second, better opportunity. Know that when you reject that which doesn't serve you, with gratitude and complete trust, something aligned with you will show up in its place.

I'm so excited that this book is already supporting people. By now, you have uncovered your awareness powers. You can now bring this skill full-circle into your self-coaching practice, entrepreneurship, relationships, and whatever obstacles and challenges you are currently facing and working through. Now, I want to gift you what is considered advanced work and will support anything you face in life. A few everyday situations or frustrations to address via this process for alignment and self-coaching angle are:

Dear _____ of the Highest Truth and Light,

"Why do I feel like I'm in a continuous loop that I can't get out of?"

"Why can't I find the happiness/relationship/success/wealth that I desire?"

"Why do I have trouble losing weight, keeping it off?"

Continue asking 'Why' after each answer you receive, until you feel complete in your understanding. 'Why, Why,

Why?' Learning these tools allows you to come back to this process throughout life's ups and downs. Situations will occur in your life, like a breakup, move, or other life-changing event. Transitions are the perfect time to go through this book again and get yourself aligned to the new life you are creating.

My phenomenal executive coach, Julien Adler, shared a story and metaphor about something as simple as a flashlight.

Imagine you are in a large warehouse with no light and millions of items. The game is that you only have a few minutes to grab what you want, and then it's yours. Because it's so dark, you only see the objects your flashlight is pointing at. There could be a treasure chest full of millions of dollars, or your favorite Classic E-Type Convertible Jaguar. Maybe a brand new camera, new computer you could use, and fully paid tickets to a phenomenal family vacation. They are all yours for the taking.

You get inside and shine your flashlight, which illuminates an old red Etch-a-Sketch, and some empty shelves. You turn frantically, thinking this is unproductive, as the flashlight only picks up on some junky trinkets, so you leave.

A positive thinking individual, who's highly vibrating, fully aligned, joyous, and intentional, goes into the same warehouse with the flashlight and finds the fabulous vintage car with the treasure chest right behind it. He places the treasure chest in the back of the car, turns the headlights on, and finds more treasures worth taking! He blissfully drives out of the warehouse with a car full of precious items.

The warehouse represents the world we are in and the flashlight is our eyes. We only see what we can comprehend and are aware of. As you become more present and open to new possibilities, the flashlight will become more like a floodlight. Your light and lens expand.

Have you heard the story of the man who broke the four-minute mile record? During years everyone thought it was impossible, until one man did it. As soon as running in under four minutes was considered a possibility, the mental barrier crushed. Now, many athletes can run at that time.

Always be open to dissecting those negative patterns, being curious about where they're stemming from. You can de-program your past influences. Once you acknowledge the reasons, you can step into guided action to make peace. Learn the necessary lessons you have consciously chosen to shift your life's path.

Don't be like me, reading my journal eight years after writing it, and realizing I had wanted out of a relationship for the majority of it. I wasn't even aware that I felt that way. Awareness can lead you to take aligned action and go about your life in a more seamless, beautiful, and comprehensive way. The little things won't ruffle your feathers nearly as much and negative situations might even make you smile because you recognize the love that is there for you to receive.

I have come to realize that many retired individuals go through a process of depression when they first leave their jobs. Then, they slowly begin to understand their new truth. They have a newfound confidence in who they are through the joy of being free. Hanging with my friend and her recently retired Dad, I was impressed that he was such a goofball, dancing, smiling, and happy individual. My friend said it was as if he had finally figured out who he was. I think about my Dad and feel he's also the most joyful I've ever seen him, living his best life after retiring. He is choosing what he wants to get involved in, instead of being pressured or forced to do something else. Now it is up to them to select their joyous experience.

However, there is no reason to wait until you retire from work or other responsibilities to find your truth and joy. Find alignment and harmony now, internally. By discovering and understanding your Truth, through body intelligence, via the exercises in this book, you'll find yourself fully aligned and in a slew of magical, synchronistic moments.

There's no reason to hold back, be unabashedly you. Grow leaning, like a tree towards the sun, as it feeds its soul. Your soul is limitless. Possibilities are infinite. Listen to your body intelligence and follow it. Don't hesitate, even if it means being an awkward tree, leaning sideways and twisted as it KNOWS precisely where it needs to go to live fully aligned with the Universe. Your body also KNOWS where to go. Be light. Be in truth.

ABOUT THE AUTHOR

Bethany Londyn is a true catalyst for others. However, it starts with herself. She followed her passion for supporting people in Los Angeles, the City of Angels, diving deep into the world of personal development. She became certified as a transformational trainer and started owning her intuitive abilities. Since then, she has been leading workshops, trainings, speaking, healing, and offering Alignment Catalyst Coaching.

Londyn practices spiritual healing and intuitive personal development coaching for those aspiring to reach a new level in their life. She is determined to spread awareness that everyone recognize that they have the possibility of achieving their dreams.

Before meeting with her clients for a coaching session, she meditates to receive guidance from the Divine, to see how she can serve them best. She doesn't call herself a psychic, as she's asking specific questions for specific answers. During consultations, Londyn uses her honed skills of listening to her gut so that she can speak from intuition, and this provides action steps leading to results with her clients. Divine guidance and intuition support people in bridging the gap between their dreams and reality. Londyn knows that everyone can tap into it, and here lies the message of this book.

Outside of the spiritual space, Bethany has spent over a decade in entrepreneurial-based management & sales positions within the finance and real estate sectors, built up a real estate portfolio, and taken part in a couple of startups over the past few years. She has increased market share at her companies by creating strategic marketing plans and business relationships. Londyn holds a Bachelor of Science in Business Finance from Portland State University.

Londyn has her own consulting firm: Londyn Heights LLC, through which she supports what she is most passionate about: empowering individuals to live their truth, achieving startup growth, and conscious and connected human capital for client companies.

Companies and CEOs hire her when they have significant decisions to make, and wish to have aligned, energetic work spaces, projects and employees. You will also find her doing energetic healings and bringing intentional energetic art for her real estate clients.

In her free time, Bethany creates energetic intentional art through paintings and stays active by participating in anything the great outdoors has to offer.

If you are curious to know more, Bethany Londyn has been putting regular content out on Facebook, YouTube, Instagram, and more. Follow her or check out her website BethanyLondyn.com for updates.

I pray this book brought up some new awarenesses and inspired action to accomplish your dreams!

I would absolutely love if you enjoyed this book, to take a moment and share your thoughts on where the book supported transitions and life at online at vendors such as <u>*Amazon*</u>*,* <u>*Barnes & Noble*</u>*, and* <u>*GoodReads*</u>*.*

Also, *feel free to share with me as well, what has shifted for you since we started this journey together. Don't hesitate to tag me and let me know. I love amazing success stories!*

Blessings on Blessings!

~ Bethany Londyn

www.BethanyLondyn.com
Instagram: @BethanyLondyn
YouTube: <u>YouTube.com/BethanyLondyn1</u>

Made in the USA
Monee, IL
24 November 2019

17391486R00134